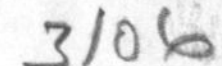

Ed Okonowicz

Myst and Lace Publishers, Inc. Elkton, Maryland

Terrifying Tales of the Beaches and Bays
First Edition

ISBN 1-890690-06-6

Published by
Myst and Lace Publishers, Inc.
1386 Fair Hill Lane
Elkton, Maryland 21921

Printed in the U.S.A.
by Victor Graphics

Photography, Typography and Design
by Kathleen Okonowicz

Dedications

To Jackie LaGuardia McCabe and Mike McCabe,
with whom I enjoy performing;
and to Mike Dixon,
my partner during our history and
cemetery walks and a true believer.
Ed Okonowicz

To Howard Burgoon, my uncle,
and in memory of his wife,
my Aunt Doris.
Kathleen Burgoon Okonowicz

Acknowledgments

The author and illustrator appreciate
the assistance of those
who have played an important role
in this project, including

John Brennan

Barbara Burgoon

Marianna Dyal

Sue Moncure

Jerry Rhodes and

Ted Stegura

for their proofreading and suggestions.

Also available from Myst and Lace Publishers, Inc.

Spirits Between the Bays Series

Volume I
Pulling Back the Curtain
(October, 1994)

Volume II
Opening the Door
(March, 1995)

Volume III
Welcome Inn
(September, 1995)

Volume IV
In the Vestibule
(August, 1996)

Volume V
Presence in the Parlor
(April, 1997)

Volume VI
Crying in the Kitchen
(April, 1998)

Volume VII
Up the Back Stairway
(April, 1999)

Volume VIII
Horror in the Hallway
(September, 1999)

Volume IX
Phantom in the Bedchamber
(June, 2000)

DelMarVa Murder Mystery Series

FIRED!
(May, 1998)

Halloween House
(May, 1999)

Stairway over the Brandywine
A Love Story
(February, 1995)

Possessed Possessions
Haunted Antiques, Furniture and Collectibles
(March, 1996)

Possessed Possessions 2
More Haunted Antiques, Furniture and Collectibles
(September, 1998)

Disappearing Delmarva
Portraits of the Peninsula People
(August, 1997)

Terrifying Tales of the Beaches and Bays
(March, 2001)

Table of Contents

True Stories

Introduction

Whether you spend the summer "at the beach" or "on the shore," whether your vacation retreat overlooks crashing ocean waves or a view of the stillness of a deep mountain lake, there's a fascination with what lies beneath the surface of the water.

At night, take a walk along the ocean shoreline and release your mind from the pressing business of the day. Cleanse your mind of thoughts about where to dine, what souvenirs remain to be bought and which amusement rides are on the coming day's list.

In the solitude of night, let your imagination take center stage, and dare to wonder what could be lurking out of sight, beneath the blackness of the water. What may have crossed the sand—at the exact spot you are standing—centuries, decades, weeks, or only a few hours or moments, before?

Indians viewing the white settlers' wooden ships for the first time.

Pirates hauling treasure chests ashore.

A drowned corpse washing up on the beach following a boating accident.

Or a lifeless drunken sailor landing ashore after being tossed overboard during a storm at sea.

And don't forget the unlucky victims of shipwrecks.

Some of them, too, eventually ended up on the coastlines of today's summer resorts. If you close your eyes, you can almost see their bloated bodies and the fast moving human scavengers, who raced out toward the surf with lanterns and torches in hand to be the first to raid the fresh corpses' pockets and steal their clothes.

Hours later, seabirds and sand creatures arrived to peck at naked skin—until nothing was left but bare, pale bones that the sea eventually reclaimed as its own.

The stories in *Terrifying Tales of the Beaches and Bays* are set in such locales as a suburban backyard and a busy seaside resort. They occur on isolated islands, near historical sites, on boats at sea and at long-forgotten mariners' graveyards. I've tried to make these stories unsettling and surprising. In this new book, I present 11 original tales. Some are based on legends or folklore, and the rest are the product of my own vivid imagination. There also is a chapter of sea superstitions I've collected over the years.

The last portion of the book includes two water-related incidents that I experienced. These, and a story by my friend Andy Ercole, are the only three true stories in this volume, and what you will read actually occurred. While Andy's story is quite inspirational, I consider my two chapters a dessert dish of humor to follow the horrifying main course.

There's an old saying that proclaims: "Man will not rest until he is buried in the ground." If that statement is true, then there are quite a few restless spirits swimming in the deep. If their main objective is to reach land, and you happen to be strolling the shore when they arrive, you could experience your very own encounter with the unknown.

Until that occurs, you can read what just might have happened to others, who got more than they expected during their summer vacation at the beach or during a weekend getaway along the bay.

—Ed Okonowicz
Spring 2001

Author's note: The next book of true Mid-Atlantic ghost stories is currently being written.

Pilot Donovan's Last Trip

On the Delaware River

Donovan was alone, resting comfortably in the River Pilot Association lounge, located on the third floor of the office/hotel complex, two blocks south of Broad Street in Center City Philadelphia.

It was the morning of New Year's Eve 1999. Less than 18 hours remained in the 20th century, and already those planning to take part in the wild midnight celebration to welcome the next century were counting down.

Two pilots, who had just arrived from guiding a tanker and container ship up the Delaware River to the Port of Philadelphia, entered the room and shouted greetings in Donovan's direction.

"Happy New Year, Dov!" the shorter and younger man of the pair called out.

Donovan turned, offered a slight nod, and returned his eyes to the brim of his coffee cup. *What the hell's happy about it?* he wondered to himself, but forced himself to remain quiet and keep his opinion in check.

Josh, the older pilot, decided to tease his old friend. "What's a matter, Dovvy? Pissed off 'cause you're stuck here on call and can't go out and tie one on?"

Twisting his large frame and white-bearded face so he could stare at the speaker, Donovan lifted his cup and offered a silent toast. Then, shaking his head slowly, answered, "Well, Mister Shit-for-Brains, when you're out there tonight, payin' 10 bucks for a draft beer and unable to find an empty seat to set your fat behind down on, and your flat feet are numb and aching, I want you to think of me. I'll be right here, warm and relaxed, with no aggravation. Just watching the idiots on TV, and laughing all the way to the bank."

"Not if a ship comes in, you won't, Dov. No way, then."

"That ain't likely, tonight, and you know it," Dov replied. "Hardly ever get a job that will set out on New Year's Eve. I'll be waiting, just in case. But I bet you I'll still be here in the morning, when you crawl in with a pounding head and a tongue that tastes like cold horse crap mixed with hot piss."

The young pilot, who had been observing the lighthearted exchange between the two old timers, laughed and cut in. "Okay. That's enough. Come on, Josh. Let's get washed up, fill out the forms and get going. We got a lot to do before tonight."

Waving, the pair gave Donovan another farewell and headed toward the first-floor office.

The 70-year-old river pilot settled back into the soft padding of the chair, closed his eyes and allowed his mind to travel.

He had been guiding ships up and down the Delaware River for nearly half a century, since the early 1950s. Now, only three months away from retirement, he shook his head and wondered what he was going to do with all the free time it promised.

Up to a year ago, he and Margaret, his wife of 52 years, had the first 18 months all figured out and booked up solid. Travel, visits to their children and relatives, putting in a larger garden. It was a long list, but they had planned to do every item on it together. And it was going to be such fun.

Donovan had promised he would make up for all the holidays he missed, all the nights and days that Margaret waited alone at home. Working the river wasn't what anyone would consider a "regular" job. Your name was placed on a never-ending list that rotated forever. When a pilot boarded a ship in Philly, he (and there were even a few she's, now) took over the controls and guided the vessel down the Delaware River to Lewes.

There, just as the ship was leaving the Bay and heading into the Atlantic Ocean, a speedboat would pick you up at sea—as long as you could descend the

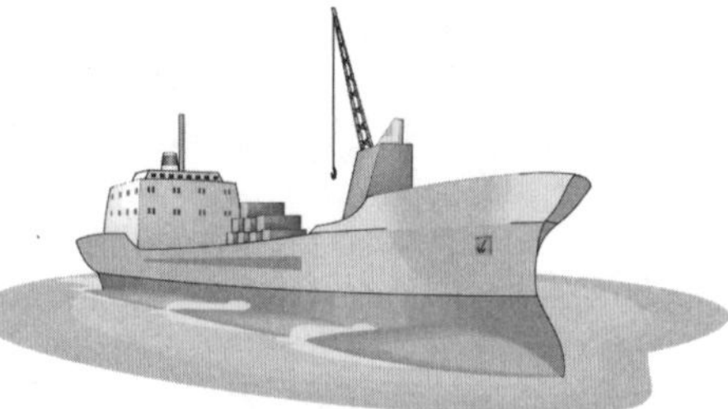

Jacobs Ladder. The dangling rope ladder with a long series of wooden steps enabled you to transfer onto the smaller boat's deck. Once safely aboard the pickup craft, you were delivered to the pilot house in Lewes and would wait for your name to come up on the list.

When that happened, you were assigned to guide an incoming ship north, into one of the docks, which were located from Delaware City in the south to a few ports north of Philadelphia.

Damn! Donovan thought, as he looked at the clock that read 0945. *It was going to be a long day. But, what the hell. I don't have anywhere to go, no one to be with. Home was nothing but a house full of painful memories. It was better to be here. Maybe someone would come in, want to talk about the old days, long before all these damn modern, ever-changing, fast paced gizmos and gadgets.*

After watching portions of two football games, grabbing a few frozen dinners and catching up on some sleep, old Father Time had advanced his clock to 1448, almost 3 p.m. And still no call from a ship.

I guess I'll be here all night, Donovan thought.

And not two minutes later the dispatcher gave him the alert over the house phone. "Dov. Got a tanker, named the *Chiltin*, heading for Norway, planning to leave outta the 33rd Street Dock about 1615. That would put you in Lewes at just about midnight. How's that sound, old buddy?"

"Like I have a choice?" Donovan replied, stretching his arms and legs. "Have the car pick me up at 3:30. I'll be ready."

"Roger," and the dispatcher rang off.

Well, there goes my quiet New Year. Like I really care, Donovan told himself. *Well, I better load up my stomach. No telling what kind of food they'll be serving tonight. I'll eat when I get to Lewes.*

It was during his first year on the job that Donovan learned how important it was to eat before boarding. When he trained new apprentice classes, he told them, "When you're on that bridge, you can't leave it for at least seven hours. You can't hit the toilet, you can't take a break, you can't even sit down. You are the one responsible for a thousand-foot-long freighter filled with oil, or a container ship with enough bananas and fruit to fill a hundred supermarkets. If you're in the bathroom and it runs aground or causes a spill, it's gonna be a lotta paychecks before your deductions will pay off your screw-up.

"And, never eat in the dark. If you're starving and you want to sample their cuisine, look at it in the light first. I know. Let me tell you, there's nothing worst than the taste of bloody chicken in the middle of the night."

The car was right on time, waiting for him at the curb. Donovan got in the front seat and tossed his overnight pack in the back.

"Happy New Year, Dov!" Harry said, offering his right hand to the pilot.

"You, too, Harry," Dov replied. "Ain't this a kick in the behind? Got one on New Year's Eve."

"Yeah! But think of the two days off you'll get next week, when the rest of the drunks are slavin' away. Anyway, how ya holdin' up, my man?"

Harry had been driving for the association for more than 15 years. A retired Philly cop, he and Donovan had hit it off from the start. They had shared a lot more than idle chatter during their drives to and from the docks.

"Sometime's it's good and other times . . . well, you know."

"Yeah. I hear ya. I took it hard when Shirley died. Hit the sauce. Depressed. Holed up in the house for a few weeks. Kicked anybody out who tried to help. Then my son came over, picked me up in the air, tossed me in a tub of ice water and threatened to beat the shit outta me." Then, laughing at the memory, Harry added, "And that helped. Pulled me back. But it was still tough. Takes time. You'll see. Just hang in there."

"I know," Dov said. Then, pausing, he added, "It's just that it's a little rougher today. See. We were married on New Year's Eve. This would have been a special night. Margaret, she always talked about us sharing the new century together, even if it was just watching the TV parties. I was going to take off. But, when she died, I just couldn't stay home, tonight. So I switched with one of the younger guys. Figured, why not?"

Harry didn't talk. They were stopped at a red light. Then, before he had a chance to reply, a teenager hit the right side of the sedan with an empty soda can. When the two men turned to locate the thrower, they spotted a half dozen delinquents, dressed in oversized clothing.

Donovan had often discussed with his wife the amazing fact that fashion designers have gotten rich by convincing weak minded kids and their equally stupid parents that baggy, overpriced rags are the fashionable thing to buy.

Margaret would reply by informing her husband that he should never be amazed at how modern parents are unable to raise their children and how they spend their money on anything TV advertisers suggest.

"Ya know, Dov," Harry said. "If this was 10 or 15 years ago, I woulda chased those little bastards down and beat the livin' shit outta them. An' look, today, here I am, as calm as can be, smilin' back at them. An' I seen this crap happen so much, I don't give a tinker's damn. Ain't that somethin'?"

"What are you going to do, Harry? Take them to the police? They'd just laugh at you and the damn kids' parents would sue your sorry ass. It's a shame, but this is the world we have to live in. It's rude. Ignorant. Stupid. We aim for the lowest common denominator. We don't reward excellence any more. And it's not just the kids, but their parents, too. None of them have any manners, not to mention any common sense. To tell you the truth, I'm glad I'll be checking out soon."

Harry waved his hand. "Cut that shit out!"

"No. I mean it," Dov replied. "I've had a pretty good run. Can't complain too much. What's left for me, anyway? Margaret's gone. We never were blessed with any kids. God knows we tried. My brothers and sisters are all dead and long gone. Hell, Harry, when I kick off, the only people at my funeral will be those who get a day off with pay."

Harry shook his head. "I'm sorry, Dov. But, ya know, I hate to have to agree with ya, but you're probably right." Then suddenly lowering his voice, he asked, "Next time you're up at the office, could you find out if I get a day off, Dov?"

Smiling, Dov replied, "Hell, Harry, I'm sure you will. I already put you in my will."

"No shit! Really? What am I gettin'?"

"Getting?" Dov asked, grinning. "You're not getting anything. I got you down to drive the damn hearse!"

Just as the two men's laughter exploded against the interior limits of the car, Harry pushed on the brake and announced, "Here your are, your majesty. Delivered safe and sound."

"Thanks, Harry. See you around," Dov said, shaking the driver's hand.

"Yeah. See ya 'round, Dov. Take it easy, now, an' Happy New Year!"

"Happy New Year to you, Harry."

The bridge of the *Chiltin* was dark, but at least it was warm. Donovan found the ship's captain to be both cordial and competent.

Because the pilots essentially took over complete control of the ship for the lengthy trip downriver to the ocean, they sometimes—not often, but on occasion—ran into a ship's captain who resented the stranger's authority.

When this occurred, the seven-hour trip became an unpleasant, never-ending ordeal.

But not this time.

Jason Brigs, as the *Chiltin's* captain, immediately informed Donovan that he was a British subject by birth but now resided in Portugal, the ship's home port. That's where they were bound.

After several hours at the wheel, Donovan felt comfortable with the progress of the trip and turned away from the radar and gauges to check his portable global positioning scanner. The GPS, which was linked to a series of satellites, indicated the ship's location within two meters. And while such an instrument was incapable of being imagined when he first became a pilot, today, in the high-tech age, it was SOP—standard operating procedure—just another crutch to make life easier, more accurate, but also more complicated.

Donovan knew, however, if the power ever went out, if the metal birds fell from the sky, if there was a nuclear accident at the Salem Nuclear Power Plant on New Jersey's Artificial Island and if the GPS went down, he and a handful of other old timers would survive. Without missing a beat, they could shift their attention to the range lights and coastal signals and guide the ships to port.

But, that would never be necessary. Not in the new Millennium. But within the hour, Donovan's entire body reacted with a shudder when he noticed that the GPS screen was blank. Responding automatically, he hit his open palm against the side of the black plastic case, but no lights or numerals reappeared.

That's strange, he thought, turning toward Brigs, who had moved alongside the pilot.

"Something wrong?" the captain asked, his crisp accent was matter of fact, not telegraphing any sense of alarm.

"I don't know," Donovan replied. "GPS is down. Might just be a temporary malfunction. I better check on it." Reaching into his duffel bag to call the dispatch office, the pilot pulled out his cellular phone. But it, too, did not respond as he pressed his fingertips against the buttons. "Must be some kind of temporary depression," Donovan said, tossing the phone onto the chair. "I'll check again in a few minutes."

Nodding, Brigs walked toward the far wall and asked, "Mind if I put on some music, Pilot Donovan? Help bring in the New Year?"

"No, fine. Go ahead. How much time do we have before the magic hour?"

"It's close to 2300 hours, 11 o'clock," Brigs said. "We're only about an hour away from Lewes. Interesting," Brigs added after a pause, "you might be celebrating with us or on shore. What do you think?" The British captain turned on some music as he stared at the pilot, waiting for an answer.

"Doesn't matter to me," Donovan said, shrugging his shoulders. "New Year's is just another day. Never had much to celebrate."

"Really?" Brigs asked, as the sound of a big band playing light swing music drifted slowly across the bridge.

Donovan, who for several seconds had been focusing on the tune in the background, caught up with Brigs' question and replied quietly, "Yeah, just a regular day."

"But it wasn't so regular in 1947, was it?"

Donovan's head turned slowly, in synch with his mind that was deliberately and carefully trying to understand where the conversation was heading. "What do you know about 1947?"

Brigs, whose uniform seemed crisper than it had appeared earlier in the evening, smiled and answered, "Oh, I think you know what happened on New Year's Eve that year, Donovan. Something to do with a wedding?"

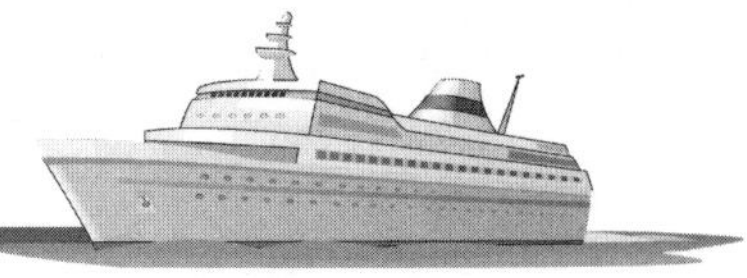

"How the hell do you know about my damn wedding?"

"Don't get upset, Donovan," Brigs said, walking closer and offering a reassuring smile. "Relax, everything is fine."

"What's that?" Donovan asked, referring to the old fashioned commercial that had come on after the song. "That's not a CD."

"CD? What's in God's name is a CD, Donovan? It's just my radio playing?"

"Radio? What station plays that kind of music anymore?"

"All of them, Donovan. All of them feature the big bands, mostly Yank musicians, as you might expect. They're on every night, you know, not just on New Year's Eve."

Putting his hand to his brow, Donovan shook his head and closed his eyes. When he opened them, the confused pilot focused on Brigs, who seemed to be wearing a different uniform. Bright white, with gold braid. Different from the khaki and green clothing he had been sporting when Donovan had boarded the ship in Philly.

"When did you change?"

"Change?" Brigs asked.

"Your uniform. That's not a tanker captain's attire," Donovan snapped.

"Tanker? What tanker. This is a cruise ship, Donovan. *USS Columbia,* bound for San Francisco. We're heading through the Panama Canal and up the West Coast. Be there in six days."

"Bullshit! This is a Portuguese tanker, headed for Venezuela. I have it right here in my . . . ."

"Your what, Donovan?"

"My log. It was suppo . . . ."

Becoming dizzy, Donovan started to stagger. Reaching out, he headed for the chair where he had left his GPS, but the case was gone. The seat was empty. He didn't care.

"Is he all right?" It was the voice of the first mate, who had arrived at the captain's side.

"I'm sure he'll be fine. He's just excited about his first cruise. Go down and tell his wife we're done with the tour her husband requested and we'll deliver Mr. Donovan to their cabin soon. She can expect him there within the next 10 minutes."

"Right, sir!"

Donovan heard the conversation, but he couldn't move. Didn't dare believe what was taking place. It was New Year's Eve 1999.

He was on the tanker *Chiltin*, not the ocean liner *Columbia*. His wife was dead, not alive, not waiting for him in their cabin.

He tried to open his eyes, but couldn't lift the lids. They were sealed shut. He was unable to move his body. Donovan could barely hear what was taking place around him, but he could sense the soft, civilized music in the background, heard the announcer say it was only 20 minutes until New Year's Eve. New Year's Eve and the beginning of 1948.

1948!

"Sir! Captain Brigs, sir!" It was a young voice calling out from the doorway to the bridge.

"Yes?"

"Mr. Donovan's wife, sir. She said to be sure you get him back to the cabin before midnight, since it's their wedding night, sir. Their honeymoon. She doesn't want to miss bringing in the New Year with her new husband."

"No problem, Mr. Sharp. Tell Mrs. Donovan her husband will be there with plenty of time to spare."

Donovan knew he was dreaming. *That's why I can't open my eyes. But maybe I don't want it to be a dream. That's why I won't open my eyes, why I'm keeping them closed. As long as I stay in this dream, there's a chance this is real. The minute I open them, it's all over. And any slight chance of seeing Margaret again is gone. So I'll just keep . . . .*

"What the hell's his problem?" the raspy voice asked. "Had too much to drink already?"

Good God in heaven, Donovan thought. *I know that voice. It's Crooked John Hatch, the dirtiest card player of all the river pilots on the Delaware. He was past retirement when I was an apprentice. I lost many a paycheck to that no good bast . . . . Damn! He's dead! Been dead for more than 20 years. How the hell did he get in here?*

"You're not supposed to have any damn guests on the bridge, ya know, captain. Better get that stinkin' drunk outta here, before somebody else comes in and catches him," Hatch snarled. "Personally, I don't give a shit, but rules is rules."

"Of course," Brigs snapped, his crisp accent as sharp and fine as his starched whites. "Take him down below. And tell his wife he'll be fine. Just got a little seasick, is all."

Donovan felt as if he had been drugged. He wondered where he was going, who he was going to see. *What happened to my equipment, my phone, the GPS. When did Hatch come aboard? Did they call for another pilot to guide the* Chiltin *when I got sick? But how did Hatch get there? This is crazy, Crooked John couldn't be there. He's not alive.*

Eventually, Donovan gave up the fight, fell asleep, had no idea where he was. Until he heard the countdown.

TEN!

The crowd was cheering in the background.

NINE!

The music was getting louder.

EIGHT!

He felt a soft feminine hand stroke his forehead.

SEVEN!

Static broke up the music and interfered with the announcer's voice.

SIX!

" . . . . are. In Times Square. . . .dy to . . .. come in the . . . ."

FIVE!

The music was louder, the announcer beginning to shout. "Everybody is eager to go WILD."

FOUR!

"They're waving their hands, shaking noise makers!"

THREE!

More music and cheering. "THIS IS IT!"

TWO!

"IT'S ALMOST HERE!"

ONE!!!!

"HAPPY 1948!!!"

Donovan felt the kiss on his lips, opened his eyes, and stared at his beautiful bride. Wanting to preserve the precious moment forever, he pulled her toward him and squeezed so tightly that Margaret pleaded for him to allow her to breathe.

"Happy New Year, sleepy head," Margaret said.

"Happy New Year, my love," he whispered, trying to maintain his composure and pray that the magical, miraculous moment was real.

"Are you all right?" Margaret asked. "I've been waiting for you for a long time."

"How long?" Donovan asked, carefully choosing his words.

"For the last two hours that you've been touring the ship. I understand, I know you're excited about going to pilots school when we get back from San Francisco, but it is our honeymoon. What could have been so important to take you away from me all night?"

Hugging Margaret tightly, Donovan answered softly, "Nothing. Nothing is more important that you. Nothing ever will be." Gently, he stoked her dark hair, stared into her familiar blue eyes and pressed his eager mouth against her tender lips.

"I love you," she said, kissing him back, and brushing her hand against his smooth cheek.

Breathing heavily, and realizing that for some unexplainable reason he had been awarded the miracle gift of a second chance, Donovan reached over, shut off the light and the young couple started their new life together . . . again.

As the bride and groom lay wrapped in each other's arms, Captain Brigs looked down toward the pilot boat waiting off Lewes in the Delaware Bay.

It was 10 minutes past midnight. However, on the southbound ship it was 1948, and on the pick-up boat waiting in bay it was the year 2000.

Smiling, Brigs wondered how the boat crew would explain that Pilot Donovan never departed from the ship, and that the tanker named the *Chiltin* never arrived. But in its place they would swear they saw a 1940s-era cruise ship, more precisely a ghost ship named the *Columbia*, sent back in time to pick up a very special passenger and return him to his waiting bride.

The One That Got Away

In the Atlantic Ocean

It was supposed to be a weekend of pleasure fishing, a get-away so the four friends could forget their dull, routine, uneventful lives. It was the ultimate outing for "the men."

Finally, the four lifetime friends had been able to carve out a time slot of freedom from their hectic, overbooked schedules. And this was it. No cell phones, no radio or beepers or laptops. No technology, except the ship-to-shore communication radio built into Todd's boat.

As the quartet headed out of the small New Jersey fishing pier, a portion of each of them wanted to disappear and never come back—never. Secretly, one of them was hoping for a ship-wreck and another wouldn't have resisted being beamed up into an alien mother ship or becoming lost in the Bermuda Triangle.

But reality would rear its horrid head in three days, a scant 72 hours. Then the weekend pirates would have to return to their respective salt mines—but for the brief time being they were free again.

The beer flowed, shots were downed, the stories they had heard for 30 years were retold—and embellished—and the fantasies they could never share with anyone else were shouted, accepted and cheered.

Oh, my Lord, life was good again.

The first day was devoted to drinking and getting there—there being a deep reef more than 30 miles from shore—where Todd said the fishing was "damn good" and "we're gonna bring in the big ones."

To Andy, the least experienced of the "crew," that meant anything larger than the half-pound fillets his wife brought home from the supermarket.

Gus and Rico rounded out the foursome. Both, like Todd, knew how to bring in the big ones.

The action happened fast on the second day of the trip, and Andy was the one who made the big catch. Sitting in a deck chair, with fishing pole in hand, at the back end of *The Raider,* he shouted as his rod was nearly yanked from his grip. Luckily, it was fastened into the metal slot at his feet.

"Hold her steady," Rico shouted, as he pointed to the way the rod was bent over, with its tip and top half nearly parallel to the ocean water.

"STEADY!" ordered Gus, adding that Andy should let out some line, give the monster some play. This was going to be a long bout, and they would have to tire out the whale on the end of the line, he added.

"WHALE!" Andy shouted, his face telegraphing a heavy dose of concern.

"Just an expression," Gus explained, laughing.

For the next 90 minutes, as Todd maneuvered *The Raider* in a zigzag pattern to wear down the prize—and Andy followed the instructions of his maritime mentors—time ticked away and the fish's resistance wore down. Finally, at midday, it took all the strength of three men—using grappling hooks and netting—to haul the 5-foot-long cod onto *The Raider's* deck.

"Jesus! What a mother!" Todd swore. "If we're not careful, this baby could sink us."

Quickly, they emptied all the ice from their food and beer coolers and packed it close to the fish, which they hid under a tarp.

In order to save the prize so Andy could get it mounted, Todd decided it was best to head for home. No one seemed to argue, even though it would cut the trip short by a half day.

It was after darkness fell, within a few hours of shore, when they came upon a stranded boat. Standing on deck, and waving a flashlight to flag them down, was a sole sailor.

Todd steered to within earshot and, realizing the man needed help, pulled carefully alongside. The stranger had a hold full of ice and provided enough frozen cold to keep the monster cod fresh until *The Raider* reached port.

A half-hour later, after Gus was able to fix the fishing boat's fuel line, the stranded seaman was seated amidst the four weekend adventurers telling tall tales of working the sea.

Laughter grew as fast as the beer disappeared, and the seaman obviously relished being the center of attention. He was from central Jersey, about 100 miles north, he said. When he lost power, he was blown off course. No one had yet responded to his radio call for help, so *The Raider's* appearance was a godsend.

Andy, who had become a fishing legend on the trip, proudly spoke of his battle with the monster.

Sailor Jack, as the new friend had identified himself, looked down on the dead fish, kicked it in the head and announced, "Damn bastards! Got to be sure they're dead before ya get too close. Remember that, boys. I seen them play possum on a deck for two hours and then take off a man's arm before he begun to bleed."

The four hosts were silent.

Then, in the dark ocean, Sailor Jack let out a bellowing laugh that chilled each man's blood. "Got ya all, didn't I?" he snarled. "Sucked ya in, just like this here dead sack o' codshit!"

Nervously, everyone began to laugh.

Except, Sailor Jack, who bent over, knelt on the deck, and placed his face a scant two inches from the fish's head. Then he twisted his head and set his eyes only inches from the dead eyes of the fish.

"I wonder what you thought as they pulled you in, you cold devil of the deep?" Sailor Jack asked. A long silver earring in the shape of a star dangled from his left earlobe and flashed eerily as it was caught in the flashlight's glow.

Suddenly, he lifted his knees off the deck, grabbed two cold beers by their longnecks and bid the boys farewell and thanks.

With one long stride, Sailor Jack bridged the gap between the two boats, started up his engines and was gone, disappearing into the invisible slit where the dark ocean water meshes with the ink black horizon.

"What a nutcake," Rico said, shaking his head.

"No shit!" Gus agreed." And did you get a load of that boat? Hell, I wouldn't go out in a creek in that piece of crap, let alone the ocean."

"*Lucky Star*," Todd added, making reference to the craft's name. "I guess he's been lucky so far."

"So far," Gus said, repeating his friend's words. "But luck only lasts so long. I guess we were his good fortune tonight."

No one spoke for a moment, then Andy added, "At least he had plenty of ice. So, in a way, he was our luck, too. Right?"

The others nodded agreement with shrugs and mumbled remarks. Finally, the four fishermen decided to turn in. Tomorrow they would make port, and the following day they would return reluctantly to reality. To a degree, at that moment, a part of each of them would have traded places with the skipper of *Lucky Star*.

The unveiling of Andy's cod caused quite a stir at the dock. All five of them posed for pictures—the four fishermen and Clarence Cod, as the catch had been affectionately named.

Andy had no hesitation in paying the price to have his prize mounted. He said he had just the right wall in his rec room reserved for Clarence's arrival. The gutting and stuffing would take about a week. The local expert who made dead fish look alive was backed up with work at his funeral parlor—there were a rash of former live ones he had to take care of first.

Andy said there was no rush. "Take care of the living first," he said, not realizing the humor in his statement.

It was while he was at work, more than two weeks later, when Andy received a call about this fish. But it wasn't the mortician, it was the police.

Officer Fletcher wanted the four men at the funeral parlor "as soon as possible." Three hours later, *The Raider's* captain and crew stood beside Dr. Christmas, the town undertaker, and Sgt. Fletcher. On the operating table was Clarence Cod—all five feet and 97 pounds of him. Resting flat on its stomach, the chilled and untouched fish looked as fresh as the day it was pulled from the deep.

"I've got something I want you men to see," the officer said, and he and Christmas shoved Clarence's body onto its side.

"Jesus Christ!" shouted Andy.

"My God!" Gus said, turning his face away from the sight.

Both Todd and Rico made no comment, but swallowed hard.

Inside the giant cod's stomach was a bloated, disfigured human head.

"I was getting ready to ship your catch here over to the factory, so they could get the meat out, but they were backed up," Christmas said. "Since I done a good deal of filleting in my time, but on a different species of meat, you understand, I told them I'd carve up the steaks. Take a few for payment, a sort of professional bartering you might call it." Christmas smiled at his comments, but no one else seemed to think they were particularly funny—except the policeman, who had seen it all in his day.

Ignoring the lack of response, the mortician continued, "So I got right in and, bam! I hit paydirt right away. I mean, I've found things inside all kinds of people you wouldn't believe—rings, that's expected, toys in little young ones. That's not unusual, either. But once I found a pair of pliers in a mechanic. Now, aside from that being part of his trade, I'd still consider that a bit odd."

No response. Everyone's eyes were fixed upon the rotting face, lying on its right side.

"But, back to this one, here," Christmas continued, "this is one for my Wall of Fame over there." He pointed to an array of instant photographs thumbtacked to a bulletin board mounted above his desk. The subjects ranged from unusual causes of death to some of the discovered objects and their human carriers.

"This one, I'd say, will move to my Top Five. Right up there with the human toe I found in one woman's stomach. But this face in the cod is a wonderful addition. Now, what remains is . . . ."

"I'll take over Marshall," Sgt. Fletcher cut in. "What remains is for us to identify this man. It's just routine, of course, and a long shot, but since you fellows brought him in with your fish, I have to ask you if you recognize him."

"How the hell could you recognize him?" Todd snapped. "It looks like a hunk of blob. Jesus, what a freakin' horrible mess."

Gus and the others nodded. They didn't know anything, and Andy and Rico were beginning to turn away and concentrate on keeping their last meal below the level of their throats.

"Christ! Can we get the hell outta here?" Gus asked. "I mean, I don't know anything. He caught the damn fish," he added, pointing to Andy. "If you need anything else, let him sign the papers or do the talking. Okay?"

"Fine," the policeman replied. "Just had to go through the motions. Check every lead. Sorry for your trouble."

As the four men turned to leave, Christmas called out, "Do you still want any of the steaks? I mean, if not, is it all right if I keep them?"

"Keep them all," Andy said, speaking for his friends. "Knock yourself out. And," he added, "cancel the order for the mounting. I don't want it now."

"That was a non-refundable deposit, you know," Christmas added, sternly. Not wanting to have trouble later, the mortician/butcher/taxidermist wanted to be sure the policeman heard the exchange.

"It's all yours, professor," Andy said. "Bon appetit."

Laughing, Christmas raised his bloodied tools and shouted at the closing door, "Bon appetit!"

It was several weeks later, after a series of restless nights of dreams of storms at sea and man-eating fish, that Andy shot up in bed, covered with sweat and screamed.

He had seen, only seconds before, during a deep sleep, a single star-shaped silver earring flash through his memory. And he knew that he has seen it two times before: Once dangling from Sailor Jack's left earlobe, and the second time, hanging from the decomposed head in Marshall Christmas' morgue.

Author's note: In August 2000, a 97-pound cod was caught off Australia's Great Barrier Reef. As its stomach was gutted at a fishery in Queensland, a human head rolled out. According to the news report, the factory owner said, "It's not an everyday occurrence that you make a discovery like this. There was disbelief. You would never dream of it." The head was fairly intact and the search for the rest of the body continued.

Heading for Home

Pea Patch Island, Delaware River

It was May 1864. Brothers Billy Ray and Jacob had been prisoners at Fort Delaware for 10 months, since they were captured by Union troops right after the battle at Gettysburg the previous July.

The island prison with its huge gray granite-walled fort was far from their home in western Virginia, but they were much closer than some of their comrades, especially those who had come from Texas and Alabama.

During the months after Lee's major defeat in Pennsylvania, the population on Pea Patch Island, located in the middle of the Delaware River between Delaware and New Jersey, had swollen to more than 16,000 souls—making it for a short time the largest city in the First State.

The brothers had made it through the humid Delaware summer and endured the bitter, damp winter cold that blew off the icy river. Unlike most of their fellow prisoners, the pair's health was still relatively good. But they knew their luck wouldn't last much longer.

They would have to make their escape soon—or not at all. And the quickest way out of the hell of a Yankee prison was to cross the swift moving river and reach the mainland only about a mile away.

Delaware was a border state, and like the state of Maryland and the rest of the Delmarva Peninsula, a large portion of the population was sympathetic to the Southern Cause. They knew if they could reach Delaware City, the small coastal community at the shoreline, they would have a good chance of finding assistance. An underground network made up of friends of the South had been established in small towns, farms and even larger cities. They had heard that if they reached the "white house" on Washington Street, they would be hidden and cared for, then spirited down to Smyrna, then Seaford, and finally onto small canoes waiting to help them on the Nanticoke River.

Once they reached that waterway, smugglers would take them across the Chesapeake Bay and deliver them to Rebel lines on the Virginia shore.

The only thing that stood between them and freedom was the river.

Until recently, it had been too cold to make their water escape, but the mid-May weather had been unseasonably hot. It was now or never.

They had heard about other prisoners who had tried to get off the island. The best tale told of three Texas cowboys who grabbed a ladder from the interior of the fort, casually walked across the moat and waved at the Union guards—who thought the skinny Rebs were heading to a work detail.

When they were out of sight around the north end of the fort, the prisoners headed into the marsh—ladder and all—doubled back to the west side of the island and used the stolen ladder to keep them afloat until they reached Delaware City.

Some said they left a note on the ladder at the town dock, stating: "Return to Fort Delaware" and signed their names and units.

While that part might be embellishment, the ladder escape caused the Yankee guards to keep a closer eye on anything that could be used as a flotation device.

Jacob had convinced Billy Ray to give up on their second option—hiding in one of the coffins that were bound for Finns Point Cemetery in New Jersey. Because the water table was too high on the island, dead prisoners were placed in wooden coffins and shipped east on barges to be buried in mass graves on the Jersey mainland.

Unless the corpse was fairly large, a desperate Reb could squeeze his living body inside the death box, and, when the detail reached the cemetery, signal for a comrade to pry open the lid before burial, and let the stowaway out.

Usually.

But that practice stopped after the Yanks began changing the Rebs on the death squad detail. As a result, a few prisoners hoping to escape got inside the coffins with the help of their comrades. But by the time the burial boxes arrived at the graveyard, the prisoner details had been changed.

Their pleadings, and screams and fists against the lids of the coffins were ignored or unheard, as they were lowered into the large hole that held the mass grave.

Jacob, Billy Ray and the other prisoners tried not to imagine the horrifying deaths of the men who thought they would be set free. Visions of frail live bodies, stuffed inside cramped coffins, smelling the stench of the dead body pressed against them. In desperation, the living called out for help. Breathing more rapidly, they used up the ever dwindling supply of stale air while their fingers clawed at the wooden lid that sealed them inside their death box.

Eventually, with bloodied hands worn down to their knuckles, they yelped their last plea, hundreds of miles from home, knowing they would never be found or identified.

The brothers chose a different option.

"It's time," Jacob said, pointing at the marsh on the southern end of Pea Patch. "Time to go home."

The sun had just gone down, and a slight breeze was picking up. The day's heat would soon be gone from the air, and the water would still be chilled, but they knew it was time to put their plan into action.

Slowly they moved out the door of the long barrack building they shared with 80 other desperate souls. But this night they knew they would never be back. They would be free or dead, heading south or consumed by the river.

"Either way," Billy Ray said, "we're better off. I'm sick of this damn place and these bastard Blue Bellies."

Every escape needs a bit of good fortune, and on this May night Lady Luck appeared in the form of a sleeping, snoring guard named Big Blue. The huge Pennsylvanian, who looked like a hog that had been stuffed into a bulging blue uniform, enjoyed abusing the prisoners. A day didn't pass without someone in the camp receiving a fist or rifle butt from Big Blue. He had been known to pummel prisoners for no reason other than they were nearby when he needed to vent his frustrations.

Victims of Big Blue ended up in the prison hospital, being tossed in the latrine cesspools and being laid in wooded boxes bound for Finns Point.

The pig-faced guard was to be avoided in and out of the fort during the normal day. To come across him during an escape attempt was certain death if caught.

With care and determination, the brothers crept past the sleeping giant—praying all the while they would not break a twig, cough or even breathe, too loudly. When they were 30 feet beyond Big Blue, they paused and their smiles telegraphed mutual relief.

Slowly Jacob's hands pulled back the large rock located where the island shore met the strands of marsh grass.

Looking back, Billy Ray watched for Big Blue or any other guards that might happen by.

No one appeared by the time Jacob pulled out their contraband—six wooden canteens. As they wrapped the empty treasures around their bodies, visions of freedom and fresh cornbread and home flashed through their minds.

The empty canteens would serve as their life preservers—the flotation devices they would need to make it across the swift currents of the Delaware.

With their shoes tied around their necks, and the canteens fixed under their armpits, the brothers hunched over and moved into the river.

Only their footprints on the short beach offered a clue of the direction in which they had gone.

"Damn!" Billy Ray whispered, "This is colder than I thought,"

"You wanna go back?" Jacob replied, softly. "I'm sure it will be a lot hotter in solitary, or under Big Blue's lash."

"Ain't goin' back, never. Headin' home!"

"Then stop jawin' and start swimmin'," his brother whispered, as the two men began to stroke toward the center of the river.

Only the rhythmic movement of their hands and feet broke the sounds of the May night. They were pleased

to be making good time, and were a fair distance off shore, when Billy Ray started to show concern.

"I got me trouble, here," he hissed, trying not to shout, but afraid of what was happening. "I'm goin' down, Jake! I'm goin' down."

Keeping his head above water as best he could, the young brother could see that his canteens were sinking below the surface.

Swimming over to help Billy Ray, Jacob grabbed one of the wooden containers. It was filling up with water.

"Damn!" he shouted, "it's been slit. There's a hole in the bottom." At the same time, he noticed that his own canteens were beginning to fill. "Somebody put holes in them," Jacob screamed. "Pull them off. Fast. We got to keep swimming without them."

"I can't do it!" Billy Ray cried. "It's too rough out here. Can't fight the current."

"You got to," the older brother ordered. "It's our only chance." The pull of the current was dragging them both south, toward the center of the river and away from shore. They had no time or energy to keep talking. They had to make progress toward the far shore, and do so immediately.

But Billy Ray had given up and began preparing for the sure punishment he would receive from the angry Yankees when he was taken back to the prison. He shouted good-bye and stopped straining against the river current.

A short time passed and Billy Ray noticed a longboat that was heading directly toward him. Standing at the bow, with the flat end of the oar extended toward Billy Ray's tired arms, was his savior—Big Blue.

"Over here! HELP!" the drowning Reb gasped.

"Comin', Johnny!" Big Blue shouted. "Just hold on a little more!"

"Quick!" Billy Ray pleaded, his voice a raspy plea.

"Take holda the oar, Johnny," Big Blue shouted, pushing the wooden stick toward the drowning boy.

Thrilled to be saved, Billy Ray raised his hands to grab the paddle and, at the same moment, thanked God for watching over him this May night.

But God's attention must have been elsewhere, for as Billy Ray closed his hands to grab Big Blue's wooden lifeline, the Reb's soaking fingers caught nothing but air.

Surprised, Billy Ray watched the oar rise toward the dark sky, out of reach. The escapee's eyes noticed the evil smirk on Big Blue's face at about the same time the wooden weapon smashed into Billy Ray's skull.

The first strike stunned the Virginian, and the second smash broke the young prisoner's skull.

Jacob, a safe distance away and knowing he would reach the mainland, heard Big Blue's sinister laugh skim across the black surface of the river. He knew what had happened, had seen it all but *was unable to help . . . too far away to turn back . . . would have died as well . . . couldn't have done anything.*

It's not surprising that for the rest of his life, Jacob would remember that night, recall his escape from Fort Delaware, hear the laughter of Big Blue. But, most of all, he would see—in daytime flashes of memory and in his nighttime dreams—Billy Ray's raised hands, seeking help, as they descended below the surface of the Delaware River.

While preparing the Fort Delaware Ghost/History Tours, this story, in various versions, was repeated by townspeople and also told by boaters, some who claim they have seen the hands of Confederate prisoners rising from below the surface of the Delaware River.

After several escape attempts involving canteens, Union troops searched the prison camp and discovered thousands of canteens, which were confiscated and kept from the prisoners.

Author's note: A reenactment of this story was featured on The Learning Channel in the program *Ghost Waters*, which features a segment on hauntings at Fort Delaware. For stories on the ghosts at this Civil War prison and its ghost tours, see *Spirits Between the Bays* series: *Welcome Inn* (Vol. III) and *Crying in the Kitchen* (Vol. VI).

The Pond

Small Town, U.S.A.

Mark looked out the kitchen window and stared towards the edge of the woods, at the site of the small family pond.

It was murky dirty, long overdue for a cleaning.

The boy hated to go near the pond. But cleaning it was his job. His father gave orders, and no one ever complained or asked him questions.

Mark wanted to tell his parents he didn't like the chore, thought a lot about asking for something else to do. But they wouldn't listen, never listened to him.

Why should they?

He was only seven. Too small to be noticed or taken seriously. He was just supposed to follow orders, do exactly as he was told.

He couldn't say what he knew . . . about where the neighborhood cats and dogs disappeared to. About where Alice, his baby sister went that summer day.

Everyone, even the police, said she had been kidnapped by strangers or gypsies. It was even in the papers. Mothers locked their door and kept their children close to home.

Mark knew what really happened, knew the whole truth.

He would get in trouble if he said anything. That's what always happened when he asked his father a question or spoke first.

The boy knew he would be beaten if he talked about the slimy, black-and-green monster—with the head like a rat and claws like a eagle—that lived under the leaves that covered the nasty surface of the pond.

But it wouldn't get him like it pulled in all the others.

Mark never got too close to the edge, and he always used the long handled fishnet to pull out the leaves—even though it was harder to work with and didn't get the pond perfectly clean.

He would never kneel down on the rocks at the edge and use the small hand net to pull out the muck. That might work faster, like his father was doing right now, but Mark knew better. He knew what was going to happen.

Staring into his bowl, he took another spoonful of crunchy cereal. For the third time, Mark's mother told him to be "extra special" nice when his father returned, be sure to apologize for not doing his chores the right way, to tell his father that this was the last time the older man would ever have to clean the pond.

Mark smiled, wiped the milk drippings from his chin. He liked his Mom. She was nice, not like his father.

She listened to him, even when she was busy and when she didn't understand what Mark said. At least she gave him some attention.

Mark liked that.

Now it was just the two of them, and as long as his mother treated him nicely, Mark decided he would make sure the pond remained clean.

Trash Rat

Ocean City, U.S.A.

Lenny leaned the weather beaten wooden ladder up against the dented, green metal Dumpster. He hated this part of the job, but the pay at the Crusty Mallet was good, and people he worked with were good. The managers were never on his case, even when the people were lined up outside the door, waiting for their seats at the popular "All You Can Eat Crabs" restaurant.

Plus, most of the chicks were decent and fun to hang with. So, when he was assigned as Trash Rat for the evening, he just held his nose and gutted through it. Besides, since it was a rotating assignment, he only had to endure the job about once every two weeks. Unless somebody bailed, but that didn't happen too often.

Trash Ratting was a name given to the worst assignment at the Crusty Mallet. Several times each night, one unlucky employee would have to dive into the Dumpsters behind the building and sort through the soiled napkins, discarded crab shells, rotting, half-eaten ears of corn and rotting chicken bones looking for silverware, trays and—although the owners would deny it on *The Bible*—unopened steamed crabs that patrons had left at the end of their meal.

Lenny thought the worst part was the smell, especially on the hot summer nights when the humidity was thick, the temperature was high and the wind was dead in the air, with no breeze to be found.

That's when the stench was the worst.

Lenny had never smelled a dead body, but he imagined that the rotting aroma wafting from the Crusty Mallet Dumpster in late August must be similar to the stench emanating off the rancid bodies of old people who die in their New York City apartments during summer heat waves and who aren't found for days.

When Lenny compared notes with other Trash Rats, he learned that the rotting smell didn't bother some of them. Others were more concerned with touching the trash, and some said it bothered them when they were inside the metal box and the garbage and insects began to move. But Lenny told them that was their own fault for looking at things too closely.

"You have to get in and get the hell out!" he said. "I time myself when I go in. Three times a night shift, and I don't spend more than five minutes in there each time. If you can't find the silverware after five minutes, it's not there, or not worth finding. Also, I shoot the inside with bug spray before I do my dive," Lenny added. "Keeps the bug movement down and helps lower the stench level a bit. But, remember, it's in and out. Fast and dirty."

That was Lenny's motto, and his recommendations to the new help when they got their first night of Trash Rat duty.

After working three summers at the Mallet, Lenny thought he had seen it all. People trying to leave without paying, hundred dollar tips, barroom fights and even a shooting. That happened the night when a girl caught her fiancee heavily involved with her maid of honor-to-be in the seclusion of the Lovers' Booth.

But on this particular summer evening, he swore he heard a voice, coming from the bottom of the Dumpster. He had just finished diving, and had felt pretty good about his find: six silver knives, two forks and more than two dozen unopened steamed crabs.

As he placed his hands on the top of the metal box, ready to pull himself out and over, he heard a whisper that he swore called out, *Help me.*

It was a man's voice and he stopped in mid-movement, slowly lowered his feet back onto the rotting garbage and looked around. Careful not to move his feet or the small bag with his recently found treasures, he wanted to hear if the sound was repeated. When no sound materialized, he shrugged to himself and turned around to leave the giant green garbage box.

Please! Help me!

The whisper was a bit louder, and this time Lenny was sure that the sound was real. Not planning to stay for a third message, he quickly grabbed the top edge of the Dumpster and jumped out.

As he turned to drop down the lid, the voice called out, even more clearly: *Lenny. Don't leave!*

That was it, and Lenny did leave, running all the way back into the rear kitchen door of the Crusty Mallet. As he threw his plastic bag on the counter, he raced toward the sink to wash up, running past Miss Ellen, an older black woman who had been at the Mallet since it was converted from an old tomato canning factory.

"What's your rush, Leonard?" Miss Ellen demanded. "Lord, boy, ya'll most runned an ol' woman over and knocked her to the floor."

"Ss-Sorry," Lenny stuttered, obviously shaken.

"What's wrong wit ya'll, Leonard? Look like ya done seen yerself a ghost, boy."

Lenny didn't respond, washed up and headed to the bar to get a free beer, and a shot of tequila to calm his nerves.

Concerned that his friends would think he was crazy, Lenny never told anyone about the voice in the Dumpster. But he made it a point to watch the other workers on the nights they pulled Trash Rat duty.

Two nights went by without any significant activity, but on the third night it happened.

Rick, a college football player who also worked as a bouncer in his college town during the school year, came flying out of the Dumpster, threw his bag into the kitchen and shouted he was going home sick.

As the hefty athlete ran toward his car in the far corner of the parking lot, Lenny followed.

The athlete's hand was shaking, making it impossible for him to get his key into the doorlock. And when Lenny appeared at Rick's side, the terrified man screamed like a frightened schoolgirl.

"Whoa! Calm down, man,' Lenny said.

"I'm fine," Rick said, still trying to unlock his car and leave the area.

"Yeah, sure. Listen, I know you heard it."

"I'm leaving," Rick said, ignoring Lenny's statement.

"Please, Rick, I heard it, too."

The athlete continued to ignore Lenny. The car door was open and he pushed the key into the ignition.

"Hey, man. Look. Let's talk. I'm telling you, I heard it, too. Come on, slow down. You're gonna wrap around a tree and wipe yourself out. All right?"

Nodding, Rick held onto the steering wheel with both hands, and then pushed his body back against the driver's seat. "Damn," he said. "It was horrible. I mean, I heard this voice, a whisper at first. Then, who or whatever it was called out my name. How the hell did the bastard know my name? And where the hell was it? I thought it was a joke at first. Then, like it could read my mind, it said. 'This isn't a joke.' That's when I dove out of there and freaked out. And I wasn't going to say anything about it. Don't want anybody to think I'm nuts, ya know?"

Lenny nodded. "I heard it, too. Called me by name three nights ago. What the hell do you think it is? A ghost maybe?"

Rick shrugged his shoulders, said he had to get home. Get some rest, try to calm down. They agreed to talk about it more the next day, and keep an eye on the next group of Trash Rats, to see if any more unusual incidents develop. "But at least we're not nuts, right?" Rick asked.

"Right," Lenny answered. "We're not nuts. Not yet, anyway."

During the next two weeks, Rick and Lenny identified three more potential allies who had acted strangely at the end of their Trash Rat duties.

Trying to keep the incidents quiet was like trying to empty the ocean with a plastic pail. Soon, employees were whispering about strange sounds coming from the Dumpster. Some tried to laugh it off, and others wouldn't discuss it at all.

It was late, right after closing, when Lenny and Rick were the last two summer employees in the kitchen. The only other worker was Miss Ellen, who had just washed her hands and was getting ready to walk home.

Lenny, who was seated on a stool, caught the elderly woman's eye across the wide kitchen counter. She had dark black skin, curly gray hair and a full figure. Her hands were thick and rough, and some claimed that long ago her fingerprints had been worn off the tips of her fingers from decades of cleaning crabs.

"You know, don't you, Miss Ellen?" Lenny said, catching her attention.

Trying to act like she hadn't heard the question, the older lady began to walk toward the door.

Speaking louder, but with respect, Lenny said it again. "You know, don't you, Miss Ellen?"

Stopping, she turned and faced the two boys. "Whatever in the Lord's name do you mean, Leonard? All I know is the sun's gonna shine tomorrow and the moon'll come back in the night, God willin'. And maybe He'll allow me to get through another precious day of hard work and toil before He calls me back home."

Ignoring her effort to confuse the conversation, Lenny stood up and said, "Please. Tell us about the voice in the Dumpster. You've been here since the beginning. Everyone's talking about ghosts and strange sounds, and half the workers are scared to death to go out there alone. Please? Will you help us? We've got to know."

"You don't gotta know nothin', Leonard. Fact is, sometimes ignorance is best. That's what I says. Now, it's late, and I'm goin' on home to get some rest for these weary ol' bones."

"So you don't know anything?" Rick asked, stepping around the counter.

Miss Ellen stopped, her face displaying the consideration that was taking place in her mind.

"It's not Christian-like to lie, you know," Rick added, smiling.

"I ain't never let a lie sneak on past these lips, young man!"

"Then don't start now," Lenny said, standing beside Rick. "Please?"

Tossing her pocketbook on the counter, Miss Ellen raised her eyes to heaven then looked at the two interrogators. "Lord save me. All right, young men. I's gonna tell ya'll what I know.

Then that'll be the end of all this ghost talk, understand? I don't wanna hear 'bout it no more!"

They nodded and Miss Ellen led them to the workroom where the three of them sat under a dim light. For the next two hours, she told them the story of Arnold Mousley.

"Poor ol' Arnold Mousley hated them crabs, hated them somethin' fierce," Miss Ellen began. "No, fact is, that poor boy was terrified of them there creatures, ever since he was a young chil'."

She explained that in the 1960s, when the Crusty Mallet opened for business, Arnold was one of the first full-time workers. His father had brought him to the restaurant when Arnold was 16, and the boy began working after school every day the place was open, and then continued all day and night during the entire summer season.

"Owner sent Arnold's paycheck straight on over to his daddy. Boy never saw a cent. Not a red cent, he didn't. Horrible shame it was, too," she said.

Even though Arnold was terrified of crabs, his father made him work at the Mallet. "Told that boy the fear was all his 'magination," Miss Ellen said. "Plus, his daddy believed that when ya'll looked the fear in the eye, it would go away. But that didn't happen to Arnold. No, sir. Fear just got to bein' worse."

The origin of Arnold's crab fright occurred when his older brother slipped a jumbo-sized, mother-of-all-crustaceans beneath Arnold's bed covers one summer night. The cold crab responded to the boy's soft human flesh by sinking its six-inch-long, mega pincher so deeply into Arnold's thigh that it took 17 stitches to sew up the leg wound. Of course, that was after they surgically pried the deadly-weapon-of-a-claw from the terrified 8-year-old boy's body.

"Well, there was Arnold, workin' here at the Mallet," Miss Ellen recalled. "An' other kids, oh, Lord, they can be so evil sometimes. One night, after cleanin' up was jus' 'bout over, somebody started chasin' the other workers 'round wit' a live crab. Well, that there sea monster is a snappin' an' clawin' away. Not doin' no real harm. In fàc', only person coulda got hurt was that there silly girl holdin' that ol' crab from the behind. But she was good at it, an' careful, too. Anyways, when she a comes near Arnold, he goes extra crazy. Hides hisself under the table an' starts a cryin' an' a carryin' on for the whole place to notice. Well, ya'll can imagine. From that day on, that poor boy was the aim of every crab joke in this here place.

"Crabs in his shoes. Crab claws in his soda drinks. Crabs in Arnold's coat pockets. An' each time he screamed, it jus' got to be worst an' worst. Oh, Lord, some of 'em thought is was so funny, but I saw they was a drivin' that poor boy crazy. I swear, I could jus' see it comin'."

Miss Ellen paused to take a sip of soda, and the two boys waited for more.

"I swear," Miss Ellen continued, "I woulda' bet my month's paycheck that ol' Arnold Mousley woulda danced wit' a live rattlesnake was if he had the choice between that an' touching the shell of a dead crab. But one night, 'fore they started this here Trash Rat business, we used t' jus' toss them shells into big ol' wooden barrels and forget about 'em. Then, when the gulls started goin' crazy, they got themselfs a big steel bin, wif a heavy door that opened and closed from the front. Looked jus' like a door to a bank vault, it did.

"So, one night, three young local fellas, they was bad ones, they was. They aimed to get Arnold drunk. An' when he passed out, they picked him up and locked him in that there steel crabshell bin, an' left 'im there for a few hours. We didn't know any o' this at the time, found out later in the night.

"Turns out, things got real busy an' the three workers, they done forgot 'bout Arnold. When they recalled he was still caged up, it was hours that went an' gone by. An' nobody'd been on out there all night, so they was rushin' like crazy ones to let the boy out, 'cause there was no latch inside, an' there they found him—all covered up wit' crab marks an' bites an' all. Was all over his body. Looked like the snappers had done an' got to every part o' his skin. Clothes was all eat up, too. It was jus' a horrifyin' scene. Po'leece had t' come an' cart him off. Bad night all 'round, as I recall. Real bad. Sad 'twas."

Lenny and Rick looked puzzled, and after pausing a moment, Rick asked the obvious question.

"I don't understand. How could there be any crab bites on Arnold, if he was inside with all the dead crab shells? I mean, there weren't any live crabs in there, were there? How could there be? They would have died out there in the heat, right?"

Miss Ellen took another sip of her soda, smacked her lips, and said, "True what you say. But there was sure somethin' in there, wasn't there now? The Po'leece say they looked all through that steel bin, an' they came up empty. Was only one way in an' out. And Arnold's heart wasn't beatin' no more. So he sure was gone to the Lord. But the question was, how did he go? Was it just his terrifin' 'magination. Some say them crabs just came back to life and started snappin' on him, like they woulda done in life. Maybe wanted to take revenge on any human flesh they could find, an' poor Arnold was the bait. I don't got no answer. But you two ain't the first to hear Arnold callin' out. No sir. Started next season after he got all eat up. Lotta activity then. Voices. Screamin'. Horrifyin' sounds. Was hard keepin' help in here for a short time, too. At least, 'til the accident. Then it all died down quite a bit."

"What accident?"

"Whole fishin' pier, where they used to have a hut out there. Called it the Crusty Rusty Bar. Well, one night, early evenin', 'fore it open up, whole little house jest fell into the bay. Right out back, there," Miss Ellen pointed toward the remnant of a narrow wooden walkway that extended from the main restaurant and headed toward the water.

"Them three boys that done locked Arnold in the trash bin was workin' out there alone, gettin' ready for a private party. Nex' thing, we all hear a big ol' crash an' come a runnin'. Jus' in time to see the whole bar an' dock crash away into the bay. Kilt all three of them boys. Didn't find them bodies for two whole weeks. An' when they did . . . ." Miss Ellen paused and took another sip from her drink.

"Go on," Lenny urged her.

"An' when they did, them three fellas was all bloated up. An' smilin' blue crabs was a stickin' to every inch o' them puffed up bodies. Had them bite marks, jus' like them found on poor ol' Arnold."

The two boys were silent, taking in the story not knowing what to say. They had asked for the truth, and now they had it.

Anticipating their next question, Miss Ellen smiled, "Don't you two go on an' keep worryin' 'bout ol' Arnold. He jus' wants some attention. Won't do ya no harm, no way. I'll go back there an' talk to him tomorrow. Calm 'im down a bit. Let 'im know he ain't been forgotten. That's all 'tis, ya know. He jus' wants to be remembered, jus' like the rest o' us."

Stranded in the Bay

In the Chesapeake Bay

In the late 1800s, thousands of fishing villages operated up and down the Atlantic Coast. Hidden in the guts and necks of every navigatible river, inlet and bay, fishing huts housing weathered men and battered boats crowded alongside the water's edge.

Only the most fearless (or brainless) fishermen dared battle the elements during the heart of the winter season. Most of them would try hard to complete their work on the water before the coldest period that extended from January through February. It was during those bitter months that the sea was most dangerous and unpredictable. It was said that a man who didn't lose his life working the deep in the middle of winter was sure to part with a few pieces of his body.

Old timers swore you could learn who had chanced getting an extra haul during the beginning of the year by looking at a sailor's hands. If he was missing a few fingers, they probably snapped off as a result of frostbite and exposure during a time when he should have stayed home, beside a warm fire.

But no one ever claimed fishermen were the smartest and most sensible breed of man. For even though they were aware of the icy water's dangers, they could be tempted quite easily by the opportunity to make an extra haul—providing they believed the weather would cooperate.

Such was the case on the Eastern Shore of Maryland in the middle of January 1887.

While sitting in the Piney Swamp Pub, four of the village's most experienced fishermen decided that the surprising winter thaw would last a week. And, if they had guessed right, they could get out into the Chesapeake Bay, pull in a quick haul and gain a substantial amount of money that would put them ahead for the coming year.

Moving quickly, they hired a ship captain, with a good nose for weather and who owned a fast boat. They paid him to haul their four fishing boats out into the Bay, drop them off and pick them up two days later. They all had grand plans to bring in a fresh load of fish and make a good profit before winter's icy blasts returned.

Captain Jim and his crew set out from the Crabtown dock and deposited the four fishermen, each in his own small boat, at distant points in the Bay.

However, several hours later, just as the captain reached the Crabtown dock, a freak storm blew up depositing a thin layer of ice across the deck of his boat. Heading for cover, he and his crew huddled below decks, hoping the weather would improve.

Before the weather had changed, the families of the four fishermen demanded that Captain Jim set back out to retrieve the fishermen.

After receiving threats to himself, crew and craft, the captain reluctantly gave in and set out in the storm to rescue the fishermen. Before darkness, he docked a second time, safely delivering three of the four men he had taken out earlier that morning.

While cheers and tears of joy were being shared among family members of the three returned sailors, Joe Fisher's family stood off near the saloon, cursing Captain Jim.

Soon an argument began, with Fisher's family threatening to torch Captain Jim's boat if he did not head out into the Bay a third time. They wanted their relative back in Crabtown.

Annoyed, Jim refused, but added, "Look. I've been out there twice already. God knows, I can't get the crew to head out a third time in one day. Besides, Joe Fisher is the best damn sailor on the entire Shore. If anyone can get back through this storm, it's Joe."

The captain agreed to leave a lookout—day and night—at the edge of the Crabtown's dock.

"If Joe makes it back up the Bay, we'll see him, sound an alarm and head out into the water to haul him in," Captain Jim said. "And I know Joe Fisher. He's a miracle worker on the water, and he'll get through this mess."

Realizing there would be no better offer, Fisher's family stopped arguing but agreed to have one of Joe's relatives take a watch alongside the sentry at the dock. And in the cold winter night, the long wait began.

In Crabtown, there was no way of knowing what was happening to Joe Fisher. More than 20 miles away from Crabtown, Joe realized he was on his own, and he would have to be both smart and lucky to get through the storm.

As the ice fell and coated his boat, Joe pulled down the mast and used the heavy sail as a blanket-like cover while he organized his options.

He knew he couldn't start a fire. Even if he were able to generate a flame, it would burn a hole in the boat. So generating or enjoying heat in any form was not an option.

Joe also realized he couldn't fall asleep. If he did, he would die of exposure.

Finally, Joe knew he had to keep moving, maintaining the passage of hot blood through his frostbite-plagued body. Otherwise, his toes and fingers—and even his arms, legs and ears—would start to fall off from the effects of the extreme cold.

So Joe began rowing—10, 15, 18, 20 hours the first day. He had to get home, had to keep warm, and rowing was the answer. He took a few little catnaps—no more than five or 10 minutes long—during the first day.

But on the second day, when the wind blowing off the water seemed worse than the earlier ice coating, Joe realized that his hands were frozen. He could not move his fingers or wrists. Still, he had to keep moving. So he bent his arms and wrapped the oar handles in the crook of his inner elbows.

And then he rowed, very slowly. While Joe wasn't making good time or distance, he knew he was alive. And that amazing fact got Joe Fisher through the second day.

On the third morning, Joe's body was numb, his hands were frozen open solid and he couldn't bend his elbows. Both arms were as straight as a pair of ironing boards. And while his eyebrows and hair were solid white and covered with a coating of ice, Joe decided he had only one chance left to make it back to Crabtown.

Joe took his stiff arms and numb hands, looked over the side of the rowboat into the icy Chesapeake, twisted his freezing body, and finally dipped both hands into the waters of the Bay.

Not feeling any pain or cold, he waited a few seconds, pulled out his dripping hands and pressed them against the ice coated oar handles.

When they were frozen in place, Joe rocked back and forth. Each rocking motion became a rhythmic stroke that he prayed would move him closer to home. Alone on the frigid Bay, Joe aimed his boat for Crabtown.

Granted, he wasn't making good time, but Joe realized that with every stroke he was still alive, still in the game, still a player—albeit a frozen one.

As dusk arrived of the third day after Joe's departure, the storm had ended. The lookout at the town dock, who was supposed to keep watching for Joe—was resting, half asleep, in an old wooden chair. Suddenly, someone nearby started shouting.

"LOOK! LOOK OUT THERE!"

Several others picked up on the excitement, and soon dozens of townspeople ran toward the shoreline.

"IT'S JOE FISHER!" several people screamed, recognizing the distinctive yellow and green stripes painted on Joe Fisher's boat. "He's coming in. HE'S COMING HOME!"

Following orders, the lookout pulled on the bell, signaling the alarm. Within minutes, five rowboats, with men holding lanterns at the bows and others shoving out hook poles, headed out to pull Joe toward shore.

With the crowd on the dock increasing rapidly, Captain Jim arrived and peered out to see if Joe was still alive.

One of the rescuers tossed a rope around Joe's small boat and several men pulled the frozen fisherman toward shore. When Joe's craft slammed into the dock, two other volunteers jumped aboard and tossed blankets around his stiff body.

Fisher's family was hugging and crying with joy. But the most happy man in Crabtown had to be Captain Jim, for Joe Fisher was back—and alive. He was not lost at sea, and even if the frozen sailor died within the next week, no one could blame Captain Jim. With Joe's arrival, the captain was off the hook. Indeed, it had become his lucky day.

Several women, noticing that the base of Joe's body was frozen to the ice coated boat, began to put hot towels over the sailor's head and shoulders. The ladies intended to thaw Joe out, starting from the head down. But it would take time to do it properly. If they went too fast or too slowly, skin damage and worse could occur. Things had to move at a deliberate pace.

Overjoyed at the turn of events, Captain Jim couldn't contain himself. Pushing through the crowd, he stepped down into Joe's boat.

Kneeling in front of the icy fisherman, Captain Jim shouted, "Joe! My good friend! HOW YA DOIN' ?"

With his palms still frozen to the oar handles, and his face just beginning to return to normal, Joe could only move his eyes, which he was able to shift from side to side. Only a grunt or whine escaped from Fisher's stiff closed mouth.

"I'm getting you out of here, Joe. HEAR ME? I'm getting you off this boat as soon as I can."

Again, Joe's eyes shifted from side to side, very quickly, as if trying to give his friend a signal. Apparently, Captain Jim didn't understand the message.

Without any warning, Jim shoved his hands beneath Joe's thighs. And in one quick, sharp, upward motion, Captain Jim yanked Joe's body off the boat's seat . . . AND THE FISHERMAN'S ELBOWS SNAPPED OFF!

A half-dozen women screamed.

Others turned away their heads.

Joe Fisher was speechless, and Captain Jim was horrified at what he had done.

But there wasn't any blood, for Joe's arms were frozen solid.

The effects of his days in the cold reached under his skin and deep into the marrow of his bones.

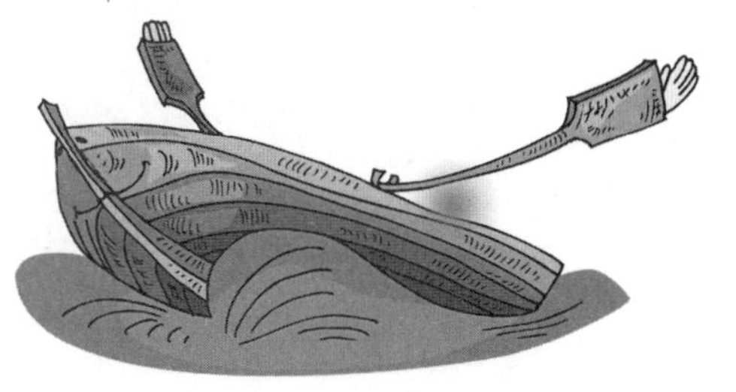

Quickly, two people threw cloths across the stumps, that were all that was left of Joe Fisher's arms, and they rushed the injured sailor into a room on the third floor of the town saloon.

That night, they fed Joe soup and tea, both spiked with hot rum and spirits. But Joe Fisher died early the next morning.

The sea had claimed another victim, and the town fell silent in grief.

Then someone remembered . . . . In the excitement the night before, no one thought to tie up Joe's rowboat to the dock. His small craft—with Joe's stump-like hands and forearms pointed toward the sky and affixed to the oar handles—had floated off unattended and was swept out into the Chesapeake Bay.

And even today, more than a hundred years later, when the few remaining crabbers and fishermen in Crabtown decide to try for an extra catch during a winter thaw, they're careful to check the shoreline for Joe Fisher.

You see, many in the town believe the dead fisherman stalks the marsh's edge, and walks along the lonely dock, looking for the rest of his body.

Now this story is sometimes called, "The Ghost with No Hands."

But others prefer to call it, "Farewell to Arms!"

Author's note: I have been telling this story at the conclusion of the Fort Delaware Ghost Tours on the Delaware City dock for the last four years. When I began sharing the tale, I would end it with the title: "The Ghost with No Hands." One day, a man heading toward his car passed beside me and quipped, "You ought to call that story "Farewell to Arms," and I'm glad I did.

Each time I use his suggested ending it gets a great response. To the kind gentleman who suggested the clever title, I offer a special "Thank you. You were right on the mark."

Lady of the Light

In the Delaware Bay

Samuel was a simple man. Not interested in fame, fortune, riches or glamour. All he wanted was peace, contentment, hard work and a loving wife.

That's the reason he joined the Civilian Lighthouse Service.

In 1880, he was assigned as keeper of Cat Tail Island Beacon, a small, stone lighthouse located on a small sandbar off an island in the middle of the Delaware Bay.

Samuel was good with tools. He could do carpentry, basic plumbing, could cook with skill, knew some farming, too. All these attributes were important in the service, for keepers would be responsible for maintaining the property and solving 99 percent of their own problems. Help and supplies were rarely nearby, and speedy communication with the mainland was nonexistent.

Samuel the keeper also was strong as a bull. When he pulled back on the oars of his dory, the boat seemed to fly over the waves. But as large and loud as Samuel was, his wife, Rebecca, was his balance—small and quiet, petite and loving.

They were a good couple, a comfortable match, and together they tended the light.

The daily chores were many, and the couple worked well. Samuel chopping wood, polishing the glass, maintaining the wooden light tower and their adjacent two-story frame home. Rebecca keeping house, polishing the brass and glass, washing the linens and performing dozens of other routine daily chores that no one noticed, until she fell ill and they piled up waiting for her attention.

Samuel had been a keeper for nearly 20 years, and he had served at a number of stations. He started his career in New England, then moved south into New Jersey. He knew that his tour at Cat Tail Island Beacon would be the last and, God willing, he would die in the service of helping others remain safe on the seas.

Both he and Rebecca adjusted well to the lonely task. The isolation was something they enjoyed. Reading, simple word games and an ample amount of conversation kept the couple at ease.

Each night, after lighting the lamps with whale oil, he climbed the steps to the top of the tower to turn the cranks of the pendulum that would rotate the light for four hours. Then, exactly three-and-a-half hours later, in the middle of the night, he would check on the lamps and fuel and rewind the crank so the rotation would continue. This occurred every night and day, and many times throughout each 24-hour cycle.

A lighthouse keeper never slept a full night unless he was sick, and even then he had to force himself to complete his duties, and they all were related to the his one reason for being—to insure that the beam was in full flare. If he was deathly sick, and he was fortunate not to be living alone, his wife or child might fill in for that limited period of time.

But such a condition would only occur for a few days, until he was well. For it was man's work and, like his brother keepers in the service on every coast, maintaining the flame became a personal devotion, almost a religious way of life.

In his day, Samuel had saved a fair number of sailors from the clutches of the sea. On hearing cries from those who had been thrown overboard while heading toward the light, he would launch his dory and rush out to find them. When he was able to pull them from the death grip of the sea and bring them back to the light, the couple cared for them until the storm would pass or help arrived. Sometimes, these strangers were on the island for weeks, even months.

When that occurred, at least Samuel and Rebecca had company and an extra set of hands to share some of the load.

Rebecca had no problem in helping the stranded, but she feared for the life of her husband. She had learned in the early days of their relationship not to offer any objections, for Samuel was pigheaded and would ignore whatever she proposed. When that occurred, he would become angry at her and remain in that mood for several days.

But in the fall of 1888, Rebecca could not hold her tongue.

A major nor'easter had been blowing for a full day. Now, in the darkness, Samuel tended the Cat Tail Island Beacon and stared out into the blackness of the Cape.

For centuries ships had been torn apart on the jagged shoals, and his job was to keep the fire going and make sure the signal warned ships away from the dangerous shore.

It was dusk, the sky was gray and the sea was hurling waves against the foundation of the lighthouse. From his post at the top of the tower, Samuel squinted his eyes to look out through the blowing rain and saw a lantern, rocking up and down at sea level. It was about a mile away, appearing at irregular intervals, but heading toward the island.

At first he thought it was his imagination, for no one could survive on the open stretch of the bay in such a storm, and no craft—whether big or small—could stay afloat under these conditions.

But he saw it again. A glimmer of flame behind a glass that should not be lit, that should not be able to stay ignited in a tossing wave of salt water and spray.

"I'm headin' out!" Samuel announced as his feet moved off the metals steps leading up and down the tower.

"Don't be a fool!" Rebecca snapped. As the words escaped her lips, she raised her fingers to her mouth, surprised that she had spoken so frankly. Now, afraid of her husband's response, she began to speak, to explain her concern. "It's a death storm out there, Samuel. You're sure to drown, be lost in the waves. What could take you outside in such a fury?"

Controlling his anger, and knowing time was short, he snapped, "I saw a lamp, not far offshore. Someone is out there. Needs my help."

"Don't go! If they were there a few minutes ago, they're probably dead by now. Perished in this storm. No one could survive these winds. Stay! Please!"

"I've got to go!"

Rebecca grabbed him by his right arm as he headed for the tower door. "Why?"

"Because it's my job!" he shouted. "It's what I do!"

"Is it worth dying for? Worth losing me?"

Samuel didn't reply, shoved her aside so hard that she fell to the floor, and he walked out the door.

The wind was so strong that it knocked the keeper to the ground. Using his hands to shield his eyes, he forced his body off the sandy surface and staggered toward the water's edge. When he reached the dock, his rowboat was gone. Only a section of thick line that had held it to the dock remained, for the fierce winds had ripped the rope apart and the boat had been blown out to sea.

Cursing his luck, Samuel began to head toward the fish shed, where a second, smaller boat was stored. He intended to use that one to head out into the raging tides. He told himself that no matter what the cost, he had to do his best to rescue whoever might still need his help.

As he used all his strength to pry open the fish shed doors, a powerful wind gust swept under the opening at the ground and slammed the thick wooden doorframe against the right side of Samuel's head, knocking him unconscious. Responding to the wide open doors and their unspoken invitation, the hurricane force gales entered the shed and tossed about the contents of every shelf and corner.

Nothing remained in place. Paint cans, tools, canvas covers, crab traps and pulleys slammed against each other as if being thrown by ghostly combatants using them as weapons to solve an argument.

Samuel lay at the entrance, unable to move and ignorant of the tempest swirling about his lifeless body. But as each giant wave landed and then receded from the island, its force pulled the unconscious keeper away from the entrance of the shed. With each rhythmic arrival and departure, Samuel's body traveled a few inches closer to the hungry sea, eager to sweep him away.

Like a patient crab with all the time in the world, over the next half hour, Samuel's body moved closer and closer to the edge of the beach. Unless he awakened, or a miracle making savior arrived, he would belong to the white breakers that were only minutes from spiriting him away.

Realizing that the storm had intensified, Rebecca decided to head out to the dock and see if she could determine her husband's situation. Even though she knew it was a fool's errand, and a dangerous decision, Rebecca tied her coat to her body, pried open the door and raced toward the edge of the island.

Since they had been in the service, she had never broken the most important rule: That when Samuel was away, she would never put herself in danger, for if he did not return it was her duty to service the light. That was her vow to him, their most sacred agreement. She knew that their love had to be secondary to their duty to the light. But she also knew that something was terribly wrong.

In her mind a voice told her, ordered her, to rush to the dock and see if Samuel needed help. And at this one time only, she followed her heart instead of her mind.

The strength of the wind knocked her down twice, and the gusts made her long skirts pull back against her body, as if they were trying to hold her back from even the slightest advancing steps. The cold rain descended in sheets, pelting against her eyes and stinging the exposed surface of her face and hands. Visibility was only a few feet.

Eventually, she lowered her body and began to crawl, deciding that she could move faster on her knees by making herself a smaller target for the wind.

Every few feet, she lifted her head and called out. "SAMUEL!" But the gusts grabbed the sound and tossed it back behind her. After three attempts, she stopped shouting and tried to conserve her energy.

Unable to measure distance or time, Rebecca eventually reached the fish shed and crawled into the wide opening that had been made by the door that had been ripped off and blown away. Finally able to open her eyes, she was shocked to find the wooden building empty. Its contents had been sucked away.

Then, lying as close as she could with her chin on the ground, she looked out toward the dock and saw Samuel's prone body, flat on its chest in the water.

Ignoring all concern for her own safety, Rebecca sprinted toward the island's edge, determined to pull her husband from the waves' grasp. Stumbling, half running, partially crawling—and all the while sobbing and gasping for air and sputtering his name—Rebecca reached Samuel's body.

Grabbing hold, she tried to pull him onto the shore, but she was exhausted and her hands kept slipping. As the receding wave tugged on him once more, Samuel began to descend into the sea. Only his neck and face remained above water.

Unable to pull him to safety, Rebecca used all her strength to slap Samuel's face, trying to wake him up, to bring him back from his unconscious state.

Twice she hit him. Then again. Harder. Finally, realizing her time was nearly gone, Rebecca formed a strong right-handed fist and smashed it hard into her husband's nose.

Already resigned to his deadly fate, Rebecca jumped in fright when Samuel screamed in pain and automatically raised his hand to his bleeding nose.

Still stunned, his eyes took in the danger of the situation and he used all his strength to pull himself from the swirling water's grasp. Helping him, Rebecca held onto the neck of his soaking shirt and together they collapsed onto the edge of the sand.

With the wind still swirling and deadly waves landing in rapid succession, the couple stumbled arm in arm toward the safety of the light. Eventually, the two injured and exhausted bodies fell through the heavy wooden door and landed side by side on the floor.

Tears of joy mixed with the salt seawater that coated their shaking bodies. Rebecca was crying from fear and laughing with delight. Proud that she had been able to save her husband and terrified of what would have happened, how he would have been lost forever, if she had not listened to the voices and went out to find him the beach.

Samuel stared into her eyes, held her close and whispered, "Thank you, Rebecca. Rebecca, my sweet love."

Holding onto him, she wept and laughed and shook, trying to force all the fear and tension from her soaking body.

"Relax," Samuel said, stroking her wet hair. "It's all over, now. Everything is fine. Don't worry. We're safe. Calm yourself. Be calm."

"Promise me," she stuttered. "Promise me you will listen to me the next time. Promise. I don't want to live without you. I can't go on without you."

Holding her face between his hands, he smiled and said, "I promise. I will listen to you. I promise."

Then slowly, they rose from the floor. And as they stood, Samuel staggered and fell to one knee.

Grabbing his shoulders, Rebecca said, "Come. Sit down. I'll get you some tea and spirits."

"I'm fine," Samuel replied, "just a little weak from all of this. Besides, I have to tend the light. It's almost time."

Shaking her head, Rebecca said, "I'll do it."

"Nonsense. I'm here! It's my job, not yours. Let me go up and do it. I'm fine."

Stamping her foot against the wet puddle on the floor, Rebecca shouted. "Damn you, Samuel! You said, you promised to listen to me, just two minutes ago, and here you are, doing things your way again. I said I would tend it, and I will tend it. Now sit here and rest!"

Nodding his head, he fell into the chair and leaned his elbows on the table. "All right, but be quick about it. And be careful."

"That's better," Rebecca said, smiling. "You tend to the tea, and I'll be back before it gets cool."

Samuel grinned and watched his wife, soaked to the skin, ascend the metal steps. Then he turned his eyes toward the teapot and waited for its whistle.

It was only three minutes before the shrill blast pulled his weary eyes toward the direction of the stove. Slowly, Samuel rose from the wooden chair and walked toward the pot.

The tea and sugar were kept in containers that stood on the counter to the left of the kitchen window. As he poured the steaming, dark tea into Rebecca's favorite cup—the one with hummingbirds painted on both sides—he heard a voice. Someone calling his name.

The wind pulled on the words and made the shout sound like it was coming from the voice of a bird. A flying bird.

"Saaam-uuu-eeellll!"

It was so sweet, so familiar in a way. So final.

But as he looked up, Samuel saw something pass, a flash of a figure, go past the kitchen window. But it hadn't flown from side to side, from left to right. It had fallen downward, as if it had dropped. . . . or perhaps *fallen* . . . from . . . the TOWER!

Dropping Rebecca's hummingbirds onto the stone floor, he ignored the crash as the cup broke into jagged white and blue pieces. He ignored the pain in his back, the aches in his neck, the bruises on his arms.

Instead, he raced through the door, charging into the still blowing storm while holding his left hand hard against his pounding heart—which was beating so forcefully that he didn't notice the pressure of the swirling wind.

And then he saw her.

His love. His savior. His Rebecca.

Her soft face looked up toward the light, at the beacon she had just finished lighting. Her dead eyes focused on the tower from which she had been sucked by the faceless fury of the sea while performing his tasks.

But she was smiling, and poor Samuel could find no reason why her face should appear so content.

For he was in such intense pain, feeling such horrifying, burning grief.

And he wondered, as he would ponder forever, why he had been saved from death only a short time before and now must bear witness to the tragedy of the one whom he had always loved.

Cat Tail Island Beacon is gone. The wooden tower, fish shed, dock and lighthouse keeper's quarters were long ago reclaimed by the force of the sea.

New, modern, mechanized lights on nearby islands and shoals now guide passing ships traveling the Delaware Bay and Atlantic Coast.

But every so often, and not as infrequently as one might think, boaters report seeing a bright light in the area where Cat Tail Island Beacon once stood. And there are others who swear, as they pass the area on certain windy nights, that they hear a woman's voice, as light as a hummingbird, calling out the name, "Saaam-uuu-eeellll!"

Gold in the Ground

Jersey Shore

His name was Captain B. That's the name everyone in Fishtown called him. And while no one knew his correct Christian name, it was obvious that at some time this local character had been a sea captain.

The short old man had a rugged leathery face, wore a dirty white captain's cap and was never seen without his carved cherry wood cane. And Barney, a nasty small green parrot, was ever present on the captain's shoulder.

In fact, we didn't know which of them was meaner—Captain B, who would snarl and mutter whenever we passed by his house, or the mischievous bird, that squawked and snapped at anyone who dared come within an arm's length of his aged master.

All of us were 10 years old, in fifth grade, when we went with Captain B to hunt for treasure. It wasn't a common occurrence. The adventure only happened once, but what a glorious event it was.

I remember that things got started on a Monday, after school while we were passing the captain's house. Since we were afraid of getting yelled at, we tried extra hard to be quiet and respectful as we walked along his uneven, brick pavement. No one enjoyed passing by the Captain's house, but it was only a half block from the school, facing the canal, so it couldn't be avoided.

From stories I'd heard over the years, it appeared that my parents—and the other guys' parents—all experienced the crazy antics of Captain B when they were growing up. So I figured that the sailor had been living in the big old house at the edge of Cherry Street forever, and that also explained his weathered, ageless look.

You didn't have to use your imagination much to get the impression that the two-story, square residence with a wrap-around porch, looked sort of like an old ship badly in need of repair. Peeling paint made it difficult to determine the siding's color. But if I was forced to make a guess, I'd say it had been pale brown when it was applied—about a century before.

A large, rusted anchor—surrounded by tall grass and thorn-bearing weeds—was partially visible in the front garden. A pair of mangled crab traps hung from a nail and could be seen blowing in the wind on the side porch. Appropriately, a signal that trouble was afoot was declared by a big black, ragged and torn pirate flag—complete with fading white crossbones and skull. It showed the effects of being left out to fly throughout the four seasons of the year.

Finally, a small touch highlighted the front of Captain B's castle. A weathered driftwood plaque, nailed to a few broken spindles beside the entrance steps to the mansion's porch, proclaimed in faded black letters: "Beware! Pirate Property."

And beware we were.

That's the reason this day was so different from every other. As our gang, we called ourselves the "Secret Six," walked with eyes lowered in front of the town pirate's porch, we were surprised when a raspy voice shouted out, "Stop! Mates, stop right there!"

And immediately, a thinner, higher pitched echo, repeated the command, "Mates, stop right there!"

We turned, looked up and saw four squinting eyes—belonging to Captain B and Barney—looking sternly down on our concerned faces.

For a moment, no one spoke. We stood stiff and uneasily, like convicts ready to be sentenced for a crime we didn't know we had committed. But, to avoid aggravation, we were willing to accept responsibility and admit to whatever the charges might be.

"Come up here, all of ya," the captain ordered. I would notice very shortly that he couldn't say anything without it sounding like a snarl or threat.

As our troop of a half-dozen shaking souls reached the top

step of the porch, the snarling owner ordered us to sit down and lean our backs up against the wall. Of course, all of us wondered why we were summoned, but not one of us had the courage to ask the obvious question: What did the captain, and his raggedy bird, want with us?

"Cat got yer tongues, mates?" he snapped, stamping the bottom tip of his cane against the wooden porch floor for emphasis.

No one replied, and he waited about 10 seconds—well beyond the time it took to make the silence uncomfortable.

In the next few moments, his cold green eyes never left our direction and, with a nasty sounding voice, the weathered seaman informed us that he had sailed the seas on wooden ships with iron men. On this, our lucky day, he was "lookin' for the makin's of a new crew, to do a little serious treasure huntin'."

All six of us were invited to sign on with Captain B for a single, full day of searching for pirate loot along the Atlantic Coast. All we had to do was show up at the time he told us and listen to everything he said. If we did that, we would collect buckets of coins and enjoy a few hours at the beach.

Smiling, we all nodded. Then one of the guys, Lenny, I think it was, said, "So do we go tomorrow and dig it all up?"

That did it.

Someone had to mess things up, and I'll never know how Lenny got up the courage to even ask a question. But the result was what we expected. Lenny's stupid question set the captain off.

Slamming the bottom tip of his cane so hard against the porch floor that it left a deep, round indentation, our host and future guide shot off into a tirade. He complained that his "crew" would get all the information it needed when he, the captain, decided. "And not a minute before," Captain B snarled as he stamped his foot and cane in unison.

Lenny's question served the captain well, for he used it as a springboard to recite his instructions.

"First, mates, if ya decide to head out with me, remember, I will treat ya all like my sons on the mighty seas. Sons of every color and continent that I nursed like a mother and protected like a mad banshee. But, I'll have me no cowards, nor crybabies, in my crew. UNDERSTAND?"

Terrified and curious, we all nodded quickly. Seeming satisfied with our silent response, and figuring we could be intimidated easily, our new leader continued.

"That mate over there wanted to go tomorrow." He pointed the bottom tip of his cane toward Lenny like a deadly spear. Then, forcing a smile, Captain B added, "While I appreciate your eagerness, and like good pirates everywhere ya seem willing to plunder the earnin's of others and benefit from their toils, but this here trip will have to wait 'til Saturday. We leave before the sun appears. All right?"

We nodded again.

As if reading our minds and the question marks materializing on our eyeballs, Captain B explained his plan.

"Listen to me, men. Only fools dig for buried treasure," he announced, smiling. Then using a thin tip of one of his clawlike fingers, he tapped his leathery forehead to make a point. "Smart pirates," he announced, "like all of ya will become, wait 'til after a storm to plunder and pillage and steal. That way, they is able to go down and lift the silver and gold coins and jewels right off the top of the beach. Ya see, mates, we let good ol' King Neptune deliver the goods straight to us."

During midweek, an immense, three-day storm was forecast along the East Coast. Captain B had calculated its winds and decided that the force of the weather disturbance would suck the long-buried treasure from its sand covered vault and deposit it onto the Jersey Shore.

He planned to send us scattering across the beach, collecting the generous gifts of the sea. After he had his pick of what we had found, we would bring our remaining finds back home—where they would be secreted in cigar boxes and cardboard hideaways for years to come.

"I tell ya, mates. After a big blow, them coins is just a litterin' across the sand, stuck in the dunes and a waitin' for ya to lift them up and bring them on home. An' that, mates, is me plan. So who's in an' who's out?

But before we answered, the captain's hand moved so swiftly that, like a magic trick, it reappeared in less than a second—waving a large, sharp, gleaming carving knife. Staring at the blade, Captain B added sternly, "Now before ya answer, mates, know that if ya ain't goin', ya better keep your little traps shut about our plans. Otherwise," he forced a frozen, gold-toothed grin and moved his cold eyes from left to right, staring each of us down for a few seconds for emphasis. "Otherwise, I might just have t' do somethin' nasty. If ya get me meaning?"

Six heads nodded as we assured the captain that our lips were sealed and that we all would return on Saturday morning, well before six o'clock. We each would bring a signed note from our parents allowing us to take the drive.

After he gave us permission, we stood up and were ready to go, but he added a few more instructions, "An' there's things I don't want ya bringin'. No shovels! No chewin' gum. It gets stuck all over my car seats. But ya can chew tabacca, though. An' none of them damn pea shooters or water guns. This ain't no day for games. This is a trip for workin' pirates, mates. Ya follow?"

Again we nodded. We would do a lot of nodding when we spent time with Captain B.

"Now head out," he snarled. "An' be on time. I ain't waitin' for none of yas. An' one last thing: Remember, there's more gold in the ground that there is in the banks! Now repeat that back!"

We hesitated.

"REPEAT IT!" he shouted.

"More gold in the ground than there is in the banks."

Laughing, the captain slammed his cane tip against the floor, signaling the end of the crew's first meeting. We flew down the porch. After racing a block away, we ran inside an alley and excitedly discussed the upcoming trip.

Would we all be able to get permission?

What should we bring?

What if there wasn't a storm?

Was it going to be safe with the killer pirate?

What happens if that wild bird bites one of us?

Can you get rabies from a parrot?

It took forever for Friday night to arrive. Josh and Tony stayed overnight at my house so we could arrive together. The other three guys said they would meet us at the captain's.

Of course, we couldn't sleep. There's something magical and contagious about having your friends in your room when the sun goes down. Everyone was nervous and waiting for the same thing at sunrise: To be sharing an exciting day, with adventures never before experienced, offering a heavy dose of uncertainty and the possibility of a bit of danger.

We all were there on time, standing on the sidewalk when Captain B and Barney exited the side door of their home. Not wasting any time, the captain collected our letters and ushered us into the car. Two of us sat in the front seat and four headed to the back.

Barney the parrot had the run of the vehicle and roamed along the backs of the seats, along the floor, under the seats and across the area below the back windshield. While he never bit anyone, it wasn't for lack of trying.

When Josh screamed after a minor Barney attack, the captain turned and shouted that he would "Stuff the next little sissy girl who made that sound inside the trunk, where the mate would be bound in chains and later dropped into the sea when we arrived."

Silence ruled for the next 12 miles.

The car, a 1960s or '70s ghetto cruiser was immense. The trunk could haul six large bodies, and the interior and exterior were a faded orange shade of bright brown.

"They don't make them like this here, beauty, mates," Captain B announced proudly. "No sir. This here chariot is one of a kind, she is, mates. The ruler of the deep himself would be jealous if he saw me behind this wheel, for sure, indeed."

We nodded and agreed. What did we know? All we wanted was to get to The Shore, haul in our treasure and play in the sand. The day was young and offered much promise.

After he parked the car, Captain B gathered us in a small semicircle and reviewed the "rules."

We were to take our plastic buckets—but no shovels of any kind were allowed—and we could ONLY pick up coins or nice stones that we found ABOVE the ground, lying on the sand.

"No one, mates. Remember this, no one digs for treasure.

I'm warnin' ya, if I see a digger, even with a twig, I'll haul yer little behind back and toss ya in the hold," he pointed to the playground-size trunk. "It's bad luck, I tell ya. So no diggin'. Repeat it!"

"NO DIGGIN' " we replied in unison.

Nodding, our leader pointed to the sand dunes and ordered us to head on over an start roaming the beaches.

I found out later that the site Captain B selected had been known as Coin Beach or Treasure Island and, at one time, Haunted Beach. All these names were the result of the area being the site of dangerous reefs that destroyed hundreds, if not thousands, of wooden ships in the 1700s and 1800s. Also, a fair number of metal vessels had been lost in the area during storms and fog, throughout history and into the early 1900s.

It didn't take us long to realize that the storm and ocean had combined to deliver the goods. In two hours, each of us had a half-filled beach bucket containing Irish copper pennies, British pence and some Spanish coins of undetermined value. The balance of our haul included colorful seashells and attractive stones worn smooth by the endless passing of the waves.

At three in the afternoon, after collecting coins and romping on the sand for hours, we were exhausted. Lying across blankets the captain had pulled from his car, we relaxed as Barney wandered nearby in search of insects and small sea creatures to devour.

After doing a head count, Captain B announced we were one mate short. Surprised, we looked around and identified Josh as missing.

Captain B stood up, pulled out an old telescope from his black coat and put the glass to his right eye. Scanning the shore in a smooth sweep from right to left, his body suddenly became rigid. Holding his breath, he adjusted the eyepiece's focus and announced, "There he is, the little bugger. Disobeyin' me cardinal rule. Damnit!"

We all jumped up and looked in the direction of the captain's spyglass. Covering our eyes to improve our focus, we could see the huddled outline of Josh, kneeling on the sand digging a deep hole.

"I said no diggin'!" Captain B shouted, as he lowered his telescope and shouted for us to keep an eye on Barney. With a speed and grace of movement we found surprising, the old man took off, running straight for Josh.

Shouting, "STOP DIGGIN'! STOP YER DIGGIN'!" Captain B tried to attract the boy's attention.

Three of us decided to run after the captain, in case he needed help. The other two mates stayed behind with the parrot.

Initially, Josh was about a football field away, but he was within easy sight when we saw him wave in reply and shout to us, "I GOTTA GET THIS GOLD COIN!" Then he lowered his head and got back to work, digging in a hole that was deep enough to consume his entire side up to the shoulder. With each long reaching arm motion, more and more of Josh's body disappeared into the hole.

"DROP THE SHOVEL!" Captain B ordered. We were right behind the captain, and much closer to Josh's position near the water line by this time.

Suddenly, Josh looked up and waved, then shoved his hand and arm down below the surface of the sandy shore, obviously making another try at grasping some sort of treasure. And that's when it happened. That's when an unbelievable sight froze the three of us like statues in our tracks—although Captain B continued to press onward.

Josh's arm did not come up from the hole. Instead, his entire body seemed to tilt upside down, as if some force underneath the sand was pulling the boy's arms into the hole below the surface of the sand.

In a few slow-motion seconds, Josh looked like he was preparing to walk across the beach shoreline on his head. But that sight lasted only a few seconds. It was replaced as our friend began to disappear, head first, into the sandy ground.

As Captain B continued to run forward, Josh's arms disappeared, and they were followed by his head, and then his back and waist. Finally, his black, hightop sneakers, with the white rubber soles, were sucked into the hole that he had dug.

The kind of hole that Captain B had warned us not to make.

The Captain reached the site just as Josh's feet were consumed. We don't know what Captain B saw, but after kneeling a few moments, the old man rose, shook his head and walked toward us. Without saying anything other than, "Let's go, mates. Time to head for home," he walked toward the car.

We followed. When someone asked about Josh, the captain simply said, "Josh can't come home. He didn't listen to orders. Now the mate's gone with them."

That was it. Nothing more, no long explanation and no groaning and tears.

The ride toward home was quiet. Although we were young, we knew something wasn't right and that Josh was going to be in deep trouble. We didn't want to admit that our buddy might be dead or gone for good, like Captain B had said. We were too young to understand how someone little like us could disappear forever. In fact, one of the guys later said he had expected to find Josh hiding in the Captain's trunk when we got home. He thought we would all hear Josh yell surprise when the captain opened the car's rear compartment to distribute the treasures we had found.

But it was no joke. Josh wasn't in the trunk. He was gone forever.

Things got crazy when Captain B stopped by Josh's house to announce that the little fellow wasn't coming home. When his parents continued to ask the captain for an explanation, the old man just kept repeating, "I told the mate not to bring a shovel, but he did. So, they took 'em away. Took the mate away for good."

Later, when pressed by the authorities, and finally mental health workers, for an explanation about Josh's whereabouts, the captain just said, "He's with the pirates, now. You can't get to 'im, ever again. They got 'im. An' serves the ungrateful mate right for disobeyin' me orders about the shovel."

Not willing to believe his story, and since the captain would never change his report or elaborate, the old man was arrested two weeks later. After a court hearing where Captain B was unable to mount a competent defense, he was committed to the state mental health facility up at Elsworth.

Several search parties spent two weeks roaming the beach, but they never found a trace of Josh. Nor was there any sighting of him in the nearby town nor in any of the villages we had passed on the way to and back from the beach.

Since we were kids, no one took our statements seriously. They thought we were seeing things when we explained that we saw our friend sucked into the sand and disappear in broad daylight, right in front of our eyes. Eventually, we were convinced that we never saw such an incredible thing happen, that it was only our imaginations running wild. As one lawyer said, "The combination of sun and sea, and a day under the influence of Captain B, will do strange things to a boy's sight, mind and memories."

We agreed that had to be the case. Nothing else made sense.

One of the captain's neighbors took in Barney, but I heard the nasty green buzzard died within a few weeks, probably heartbroken after being separated from the captain.

The old house where Captain B had lived remained vacant for six years, until he died in his sleep at the mental hospital. No doubt the old sailor missed looking out over the old canal and watching the tankers and modern sailing ships pass by all day and night.

There was no way of knowing how old he had been, but that didn't matter. He seemed like he had made a good run at life, until that day he took out the Secret Six.

I was 16 years old when I heard that Captain B had died. There was no funeral or ceremony in Fishtown. The only official event related to his life and death was an auction sale of his home and its contents.

It was on a Saturday morning in late May. I joined in with a crowd of humanity that roamed the old house in search of treasures it could pick from an old man's lifetime of effort and work.

I watched as strangers and neighbors touched and discarded relics of the dead sailor's past, making comments about his collection. Most of the statements were cruel, impersonal—flippant remarks about the memories of a stranger's life, a soul they neither knew nor cared about. They were on the scene much like buzzards arriving to savor a few bites of a road kill before it is swept away.

At times, I wondered how we were any different than preying animals. I questioned what right we had to touch and move and comment upon Captain B's prized possessions. In a small way, however, I felt closer to him than the scavengers with their out-of-state license plates, or the Fishtown neighbors who had never said hello, but had become gleeful voyeurs. Years before, they probably could have had a private tour of the captain's museum in exchange for a warm cup of coffee or homemade casserole.

It was in the parlor that I saw it, a gray, leather bound book entitled, *Pirate Life, Lore and Legends*. It was printed in London, in 1896, and Captain B had signed the front page and inscribed a personal note.

Purchased in Philadelphia, on the sunny day of May 16, 1909, by Brian L. Bloodsworth, sea captain of the Royal Wind, from James Malloy, proprietor of McLeary's Fine Books, Charts and Documents.

Could I actually be holding Captain B's signature, I wondered? And as I leafed through the pages, I discovered a folded letter. Apparently, it had served the owner as a bookmark, and it was stuck into the page at the beginning of Chapter VII—entitled "Burying the Treasure."

Gently closing the volume, I walked to an auctioneer's assistant and purchased the work for six dollars. Happy to have a tangible memory of Captain B's colorful past, and possibly his signature, I walked home and planned to begin reading my special discovery that evening.

Things became hectic, and two days passed before I was able to sit at the desk in my bedroom and open the book. Slowly, I pulled out the folded piece of lined paper. My hands began to shake slightly as I realized what I held. It was dated two days after our trip to the shore. In the shaky script of an old weathered hand, Captain B had written:

> "To the finder of this book:
>
> "The boy just wouldn't listen. Told him not to bring a shovel, nor use one out there on the sandy beach. He was only told to pick up coins that was on top. No digging, I told them all more than one time. But there's always one who don't hear, or who don't want to hear. Same way was at sea as is on land.

"So there he was. I looked through me glass, and I saw his hand going under and under, deep. I knew they was gonna get him. When I got close, they had already started to pull him down. Was dragging him under for good.

"I saw his head go in first. Saw shoulders go under the ground next. Followed right along. The last thing was them two black sneakers. They sinked under the sand. Went right into the hole like they was being sucked down a hungry drain.

"Them three other boys was standing back behind me. They was stiff, just like little stone statues, cold and frozen. They didn't want to get no closer. Can't blame them.

"Just as he was all gone, I come up to the hole he dug. Leaned my head over and looked down, inside it, staring at the bottom. That's when I saw it. The large Spanish gold piece. It was a good silver dollar size. No wonder the damn boy wanted to have it. Who wouldn't of tried to grab for it? There she was, just a gleaming in the sun, like a golden, yellow bright jewel, perfect and round. Looked to me like it just come outta the mint.

"As it sat there in the deep hole, all of a sudden, a hand made of bones, a white skeleton hand reached up, from under the sand hole. It wrapped its bony fingers around the coin and pulled it down.

"Then it was gone. All gone. Coin and hand and all. Just like the stupid boy who didn't listen. I was just ready to turn away, when the skull came up through the same hole. Looked right at me, then it went back down and was gone for good.

"It was like a signal, telling me there was nothing I could do. The boy was with them now. Gone. Gone 'cause he didn't listen. Well, that will teach him, and be a warning to others, too. They was real good in the car on the way back. Afraid I was gonna leave them on the beach for the sand demons, I guess.

"It's been two days since I told the mother. Police has been here seven times. I expect they'll be coming soon to take me away. Nothing I can do. No fight in me left. If it was 10 years before now, I might of taken Barney and lit out. But not now. Not any more. Too damn old for nonsense.

"I kept telling them the truth, that it was the pirates got him. But they don't want to believe. They don't want to hear that. Can't understand. They want me to tell them were I hid him, where he's off to. I told them I don't know where they keep him. Under the

sand, I guess. They got mad when I said the mate got what he did 'cause he didn't listen to me warnings. Somehow they don't understand that anymore. Kids do what they want so much, it's like they are the rulers. Well, this one found out different.

"When they come, I guess they'll sell things off. Knock down the house. Won't matter none to me, I'll just be dust somewhere. Hope I end up out on the water somehow. That would be good. But I got no control. Can't control what happens now anymore than parents can control kids, today. It's all out of control. Spinning down the drain, just like that kid was sucked under the ground."

There also was a hand written entry on the side of the page that was bookmarked by Captain B's letter. In the right margin were the words: "This is what happened to the boy with the shovel."

The chapter described the age old pirate practice of leaving a freshly killed buccaneer's corpse on top of any chests of treasure that had been buried on the shore. Apparently, Josh had come upon a gold coin that was being guarded by the rotting skeleton that had been charged with keeping the loot safe and sound. And now Josh has taken over the guard duty . . . until he's able to entice another sentry to take his place beneath the sand.

Author's note: To read a story about a terrifying, unexplained event involving a pirate sighting on the present-day Jersey Shore, see "Don't Sleep on the Beach," in *Up the Back Stairway,* Vol. VII of the *Spirits Between the Bays* Mid-Atlantic ghost/folklore series.

Gifted Guard

John Brown Island, Virginia, and Upper Eastern Shore of Maryland

His grandmother had told him he "had the gift." At the time her raspy voice spoke the words, Nevitte was only four years old. He had no idea what the elderly woman meant, but as the years passed he realized she had been correct.

Nevitte York could read people's minds. He also could touch things and get visions of events that had happened in the past. Sometimes, he also heard conversations. And rarely, but it did happen, he could tell the future.

He had no control over what he saw or heard or felt, and he couldn't determine when the charm would enable him to experience the power. But as he got older, Nevitte noticed that "the spells," as he called them, were beginning to occur more frequently. That's one of the reasons he had quit his job at the post office. Handling all those letters in the processing center was like being deluged with a series of sights and sounds—strange faces and places and scenes—that caused his vision to blur and his head to spin.

On some days, as he tossed single letters and packages into narrow slots and wide bins, the mind pictures would never end, no matter what he did. He knew he had to get away, had to find a simpler, quieter place of employment.

The Eastern Shore Decoy Museum and Village turned out to be the right choice.

He had applied for the position as the lone guard on the graveyard shift. With good references and following a comfortable interview, he landed the job.

What could be calmer, Nevitte wondered, than to be alone from 11 at night to 7 o'clock in the morning, and all he had to do was stay awake and call the police if he noticed anything strange. It wasn't like working at a convenience store or in a bank. Who was going to bother breaking into a decoy collection museum? After all, hocking a wooden duck at a pawn shop would be a heck of a lot harder than trying to get quick cash by lifting a TV or VCR from a residence or ripping a CD player from a parked car.

In Nevitte's mind, the chance of encountering trouble at the Eastern Shore Decoy Museum and Village was as remote as meeting Elvis during his nightly rounds. The peace and quiet of the two-story museum on the banks of the Upper Chesapeake Bay was just what Nevitte was seeking. And, as the Good Book says, "Seek and you shall find." Nevitte York had found.

He had been on the job for about three weeks and was settling into a routine. He had a firm handle on what was supposed to be in the glass cased displays, where the light switches were located, the times when he could snooze and the portions of the shift that demanded his utmost attention.

Soon after his arrival, Nevitte made it a point to read all of the materials the museum had provided about its history, the items in its permanent collection and current and future exhibitions, lectures, programs and events. He was a bit surprised that he began to take an interest in the carved ducks. Alone, in the early morning, he would turn on the display case lights and study the different types of carvings that reflected the style of various decoy making areas throughout the region.

He got to the point where he could distinguish a Susquehanna Flats carving from one made over near Cape May, New Jersey, or in Chincoteague, Virginia. He also was impressed with the early American Indian decoys that had been constructed of strands of straw and corn husks. Nevitte had never imagined they existed, and he found their presence and history of particular interest.

Having had several weeks of peace and calm, he hadn't given the spells much thought. But that's when they tended to surface, when he thought he had put them out of his mind.

About 3 o'clock one morning, he stood facing the display case filled with decoys from the Salisbury, Maryland, area. Suddenly, a flash commanded his attention. The black eyes of the tan, reddish-brown painted woodduck with the yellow tipped bill, seemed to penetrate deep into Nevitte's open mind.

"Let me out!" was the message, clear and sharp as if it had been spoken. But Nevitte was sure no sound had escaped the wooden creature nor traveled through the thick glass case.

"I don't belong here!" the decoy telegraphed.

Nevitte took a few steps back, instinctively trying to distance himself from the messenger. But his effort didn't work.

Again the wooden creature called out a plea for help. "I know you can hear me. Open the case and hold me. You'll understand."

Nevitte began to turn, to walk away from the exhibit and return to his chair in the security command center. But after taking only a half-dozen steps, he stopped, made an about face and headed back toward the troubled decoy. Resigning himself to a new adventure, Nevitte knew that if he ignored the voices in the spell, turned his back on the gift, he would wonder what message he had ignored.

His grandmother had called it a "gift," and one time, when Nevitte's mother was absent, the old woman held the young boy close and whispered, "Remember, Nevitte. You are special, and you have a gift. And when I'm gone, and no matter what all they say to you, remember this: A gift cannot be given back and a gift can't be ignored. You must be thankful for it, and you must use it."

Tonight, at the "Duck House," as Nevitte called his job site, he would see what the gift was telling him to do.

As he placed the jagged silver key into the half-moon-shaped lock that secured the glass doors, Nevitte hoped he wouldn't regret getting involved. It had happened so often before, and up to this point, at the museum, everything seemed to be going well.

Sliding the glass panel to his right, he paused, took a deep breath, reached up and grabbed the wooden duck and pulled it from the shelf. He knew that if the curators saw him holding the expensive, sought-after 1940s-era Stanley Sharpe antique in his bare hands—that contained harmful, natural body oils—they would fire him immediately. But he also knew that he could not wear any type of gloves when he was managing his gift. Cloth or rubber gloves interfered with his delicate powers. Nevitte had to touch the object or person with his bare hands.

Holding the reddish duck softly, almost cradling it in his palms and rocking it back and forth in his forearms, Nevitte closed his eyes and waited for the pictures to surface and the show to begin. He could tell from the warmth being generated in the palms of his hands that it wouldn't take long. There was a message here, and he was going to discover it.

Suddenly, his forehead began to perspire and he saw the mind movie commence.

It was summer. In a marsh. Two men were laughing, tossing empty longneck bottles of beer into the weeds. They were skinny, in jeans and T-shirts and nearly covered from chest to boots with damp gray and brown mud.

An old 1970s era pickup was nearby. It was missing a tailgate and had a black dented body that was half eaten by rust.

"Hell, Wadie!" the taller man shouted, 'jest one more to dig up and we're on our way. That'll make nine, total."

"Shoulda been 12, if ya wouldn't a lost the others," the shorter man snarled, spitting a stream of wet tobacco juice onto the trampled marsh grass.

"Ain't my fault, dipshit! They moves, ya know." His name was Willard.

"Yeah, right!" Wadie replied. "Them dead wooden duck shapes just get up an' wiggle them little ol' ghost web feet an' head off through eight feet deep o' thick wet mud, and then get up and head on t'ward the bay. All by them lonesomes."

"Hell, no! Ya know what I mean," Willard snapped back. "They shift, an' they tend t' sag and roll. Ground movement over the last six months pulls 'em over a bit from the stake and the rope or chain can snap. Hey! Nine outta a full dozen's good 'nough fer me. Damn straight!" The tall one shook his head and knelt down into the mud pulling an eight-foot long two-by-four piece of pine wood up toward the surface.

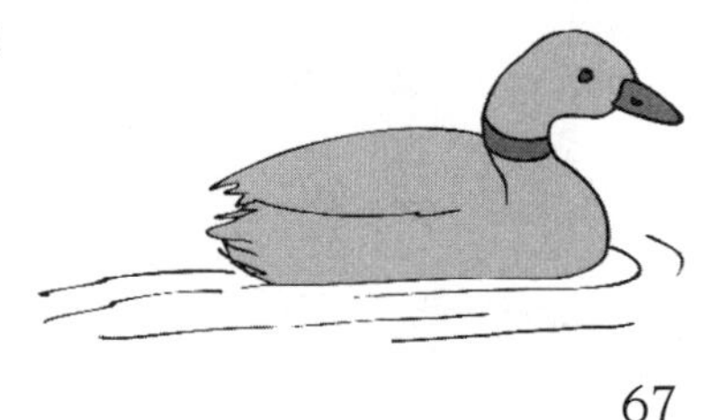

"Come on to daddy, Quack Quack," Wadie sang out. "We're

gonna take ya on home and get ya'll fixed up nice and fine." Just then the bottom of the long board broke the surface, and the last "decoy-shaped" piece of wood landed in Willard's grime-coated grip.

Nevitte held onto the museum decoy a bit tighter and shook his head. Slowly, he placed the antique on top of a nearby case and took a few deep breaths. At times during a session, he learned that he had to pause, slice out a small break before the mind movie continued. If not, the pressure that would eventually consume the outside of his head would begin too soon, and he wouldn't be able to finish the show. It was important that he remain focused until the ending and be able to understand what the movie all meant and, most importantly, what he was supposed to do.

Lifting the decoy again, he breathed, shut out the present and concentrated.

The two men, Willard and Wadie were inside an office. The scene was bright and new, an immaculate setting compared to the filthy mud marsh where the adventure had begun.

The watermen were talking to a well dressed man. The brushes and canvas nearby made the room appear to be an art studio.

"We gotcha nine of 'em this time, Mr. Chamlin."

"*Chamlin*," the younger, frail, yuppie-looking man replied, stressing the word. "I told you, I am just *Chamlin*. That's my artistic signature as well as my name. Everyone knows me as *Chamlin*. Let us not confuse the public. Shall we not?"

"Not what?" Wadie asked, shrugging his shoulders and looking at Willard for support.

The shorter dirt-coated partner just looked over and shrugged.

"Never mind," Chamlin snapped, raising his eyebrows and head to demonstrate his impatience. "It's neither here nor there with you two harlequins. I will accept the pieces, although I am disappointed since I was expecting delivery of 12. I do have orders to satisfy, you must surely realize."

"We gotcha NINE!" Wadie snarled, getting pissed off. "Ya don't want 'em, we'll throw 'em out. Don't make no difference to us, ya know. We can live without 'em. But looks t' me like you can't." The taller visitor grinned after the last statement, directing a set of jagged, tobacco stained teeth in Chamlin's direction.

"Fine!" the artist said, obviously annoyed. "But you will only receive $450. That is proper payment for nine at the previously agreed upon rate of $50 per piece."

"Nope!" interjected Willard. "We want us the whole $600. That was the deal up front. $600 or we dump 'em back in the hole."

"That is simply outrageous!" Chamlin ran a nervous hand through this puffed up blond hair. "I am only receiving delivery of three-fourths of my stated order! I protest!"

Bursting out in laughter the two men's bodies shook with glee. "Well, why doncha just call a cop?" After a volley of laughter filled the room, Willard continued. "Let me try to 'splaine our sitch-ooo-way-chun to ya. Let's just say that we done suffered what ya might wanna call an unfortunate act of God! *Mr. Chamlin.* So that's just business on the water as we sees it, see? So what's it gonna be, partner? Do ya pay us all what we 'spect, or do ya wanna wait another two seasons for a new batch to ripen in the mud vine?"

Chamlin was annoyed, but he fished out a roll of twenty dollar bills, counted out 30 and dropped them onto the table.

"Looks like he ain't gonna get hisself another supplier," Wadie added, laughing at what he considered a very clever comment.

Chamlin forced a grin and, before either of the mud rats could snatch up their pay, the artist announced, "Let us go out and examine the merchandise. I assume the pieces are on the side porch, adjacent to the fountains and Horseshoe Garden?"

"Like we always deliver to ya, twiceta year, *Mr. Chamlin,*" Wadie replied. "An' we know better than t' bring that ol' mud bag into yer nice clean office. Don't wanna leave no traces that we was here an' ruin yer fine *ar-tis-tic* reputation, now. Do we now, Willard?"

As laughter began, Nevitte shook his head and took another short break. He had an idea of where the tale was going, but he held back from speculating. He also knew that could interfere with the message. Nevitte wanted the communication to come from the decoy. Coupled with his own mental images that would complete the story.

When his image making process kicked back into gear, Nevitte reentered the story in Chamlin's studio. He saw the artist holding what appeared to be a damaged antique decoy, examining its shape and pressing his thin fingers into the indentations and jagged marks that had been inflicted on its once-smooth body.

Picking up the phone, Chamlin placed a call. Smiling, the artist waited for the person on the other end to respond. Apparently reacting to a message machine, Chamlin said, "Mrs. Bredin. This is Chamlin, at my studio on John Brown Island. I am the bearer of wonderful news. I shall soon be in possession of the antique Stanley Sharpe decoy you have requested that I locate. Please call me back, promptly so I may arrange the transaction. I estimate it will be presentable for display within 10 days. In addition, I was able to negotiate a competitive outlay at a mere $7,000. I await your reply. However, I must add a note of urgency, I have several clients seeking this particular piece. Therefore, I strongly recommend a hasty reply. Thank you and have a pleasant day."

As he replaced the telephone receiver in its white-and-gold Victorian-era cradle, Chamlin smiled and turned toward a reference book entitled *Stanley Sharpe: Decoys, Wooden Boats and Other Rustic Woodwork, 1915-1949.* Opening its pages, he began to make plans to create the decoy that had been ordered.

Nevitte opened his eyes and set the decoy down.

That was all he needed to see. He had heard stories of scams involving fake decoys being sold for high prices after being represented as originals. Watermen seeking a quick buck would copy the rough shape of a noted carver, take the unpainted wooden duck and shove it into a mud flat to cure for several months. When it was pulled up, the piece looked like it was truly 60 years old.

Sometimes they would beat the soaked wooden shape with chains to give it that distressed, overused look. Other sharpies set the fakes in the water and peppered them with buckshot then let them sit and soak.

Eventually, a skilled artist would add the right paint coating and copy the noted carver's blade style and signature markings. Unsuspecting collectors, all of whom wanted to have a "name" carver's work under glass in their office or home, would pay thousands of dollars to secure such a rare find.

Apparently, the wooden duck in Nevitte's possession was not a 1930s-era Stanley Sharpe, but a counterfeit manufactured recently by Willard, Wadie and Chamlin.

As the troubled guard gently placed the reddish brown duck back into its place on the exhibit case shelf, he wondered what to do.

If he told the curators, they would laugh at him, or worse. What would a lowly guard know about rare, authenticated antique carvings that had passed the tests of college educated experts?

And if he stole the piece and tossed it back into the river, the duck would be happy but Nevitte would certainly be found out and wind up in jail. That was a dead end road he didn't plan to travel.

He would need time to think this one out.

The electric bell sounded behind the counter alerting the well-attired hostess that a customer had entered Chamlin's Gallery, not far from Assateague Bay on John Brown Island.

It was a modern, upscale gallery, accented with contemporary furnishings and artworks. Very few of the artworks were realistic and the pieces of sculpture were bizarre and indescribable. In fact, Nevitte, who was enjoying his weekend off, wondered who would buy these God awful contraptions. But, what did he know? After all, it looked like Chamlin's was doing well and the owner was able to pay the hired help and rent.

"Can I help you, sir?" the young lady asked, looking over the security guard's casual attire and trying to determine if he was worth spending time on. After all, her commission depended upon catering to those who could afford what the shop had to offer. Lookers were fine, but buyers were better. And, she decided quickly, this one wasn't going to be a buyer.

"I'm here to see Mr. Chamlin," Nevitte announced casually.

"Do you have an appointment?" she inquired curtly. "*Chamlin* only sees clients who call in advance."

"I see," Nevitte said. "Well, I don't have an appointment, but I'm sure he'll make the time. Just tell him I'm a friend of Wadie and Willard."

Responding as if she had been sprayed by a skunk, the hostess replied, "I'll tell Chamlin, but I doubt you'll be seeing him today."

Within five minutes, Nevitte was seated in a comfortable chair in the studio where Wadie and Willard had executed their business dealings with Chamlin. After a few awkward moments, and an even briefer period of pleasantries, Nevitte explained his plan to Chamlin.

As expected, there was a very brief period of protest, but this was followed by an agreement that Chamlin would purchase back the reddish/brown decoy from the Eastern Shore Decoy Museum and Village. How that occurred was the artist/counterfeiter's problem. But the piece had to be in Nevitte's hands within two weeks.

As Nevitte exited from Chamlin's private studio and walked through the gallery, the hostess offered a wide grin and showed him more respect than when he had arrived.

It was only 10 days later when Nevitte arrived at work, made his first set of rounds and noticed that the reddish-brown Stanley Sharpe decoy was gone, replaced by a Ward brothers piece from the same era. Pausing, the security guard allowed himself a broad smile, for he knew that his grandmother was right: He had the gift, and he was supposed to use it.

Now his next task was to prepare a place to display his new wooden friend, that would be arriving soon in the mail.

Scrimshaw Scribe

Atlantic Coast

"HELL-O! ANYBODY HOME?" Teddy Bear called out. The large man with the jolly disposition stood two feet within the doorway of the neat and compact gift shop. Looking like a twin bother of Santa Claus, his clear blue eyes scanned over and around stacks of glass shelving and low counters of goods seeking the location of the store owner.

"Over here, Teddy Bear," Mary shouted. "I sure hope you've got my order. I've got customers a waiting."

"Right here," Teddy Bear announced, tapping the box with his free hand and smiling proudly. "Just as you requested, my dear. Seven pairs of scrimshaw earrings, two pocket knives with the new nautical designs and a dozen rings, each with adjustable bands of course, all sporting sailing ships in the wind."

"You are a regular machine, Teddy Bear!" Mary said, slapping the vendor on his arm. "I just don't know how you do it, and how you keep finding the material to create these marvelous pieces of jewelry. They're starting to be my best sellers."

Shaking his head and grinning mischievously, Teddy Bear replied, "Now, Mary, darling. You know, just like a fine chef, I can't give away my trade secrets. Just be glad that you're on the top of my list and always get serviced first. Have I ever made you wait for an order, dear? Have I, ever?"

Completing her signature on the company check, Mary passed it to Teddy Bear and replied. "No. You are always on time or here ahead of the deadline promised, Teddy dear. But I just hate the thought of that nasty Jenna Britch, at Britches and Stitches on the other side of town, also having your pieces. You know, I really should demand exclusivity of your products, Teddy Bear."

Ignoring the old song that Mary sang every time he visited her shop, Teddy Bear bowed, thanked her for the business and headed toward the door. "Just call in any new orders," he announced before he shut the door behind him. "I'll be out of town for a few days. Got errands to run."

"Heading off to your suppliers?"

"Got to run, Mary dear," he replied and disappeared.

Teddy Bear had lived by the sea his entire life. He loved the smell of the air, the change of weather, the soft breezes in summer and the bitter blasts during wintertime He even enjoyed the hurricanes and storms. It was the world he had been born into and the world in which he had long ago decided to remain—whatever the cost.

When he returned home from college with a degree in art, he had tried painting. But watercolor artists and oil painters were tripping over each other, capturing the same overdone scenes and fighting and backbiting to stay above water both financially and mentally. Also, there was the damn necessity to attend those deadly art show receptions, where rich old ladies with blue hair and gray skin would ooh and ahh over guys wearing makeup, who talked with a lisp and were queerer than a nine dollar bill.

Tiring of the pace, fakery and demands of the creative life, Teddy Bear made a major lifestyle change and signed on with a fishing boat. For three years he worked charters and performed commercial work. Then, one night passing some idle time, he accidentally discovered woodcarving.

After decorating a few pieces of driftwood and shaping a series of nautical figures, Teddy Bear realized he was skilled with a knife. Eventually he found a more specialized niche—scrimshaw. To him, nothing was more satisfying than creating an indelible image in and onto the bone and teeth of whales and fish. After studying the art's history, and visiting museums with collections of the original mariner artwork, he bought dozens of books and began to imitate the best of the craft's past works.

Teddy Bear was amazed at the minute detail the self-taught sailor artists were able to inscribe on such small areas. He had seen scrimshaw used as clock stands and fascinating carved heads that functioned as handles of men's and women's canes. On large whale teeth, long-gone carvers had inscribed entire villages and ship battle scenes using several different colors of ink. Pie crust crimpers, ditty boxes, corset stays and even knitting needles were made of attractively decorated scrimshaw.

It was truly amazing what his predecessors had created on whale teeth and bone.

But Teddy Bear also found that constructing each scrimshaw art piece was like walking along the edge of a dangerous cliff, because creativity had to be balanced with a high degree of care. Make a mistake while painting on a piece of canvas or paper and you could throw the damaged material away and buy more. In such instances, the artist had only lost his time and the price of the paper.

Slip while carving on a 400-year-old whale tooth or a sliver of elephant ivory and the situation could be catastrophic. With scrimshaw, which was prohibitively expensive, there also was no guarantee one would be able to locate—or afford—more material.

That was Teddy Bear's major concern—that he would run out of substances upon which he would carve his images. For without the precious slivers of ivory, teeth and bone, he knew he would be out of business permanently.

He had been depending upon a New England supplier who imported ivory and whale bone from legal and illegal sources in Africa, Asia and the North Atlantic. But more than once the importer has alluded to the difficulties he was experiencing because of limited supply and government intrusion due to pressure from "environmental wackos."

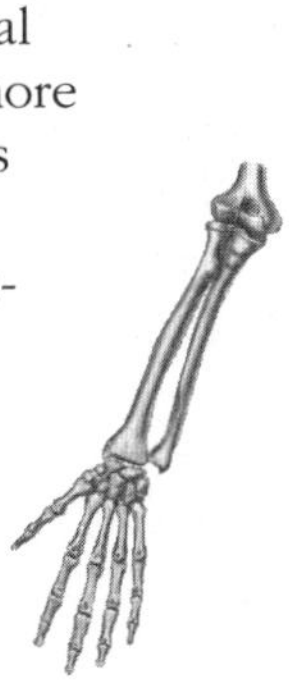

Synthetic materials were coming on the market, but they had an ungenuine look about them. Besides, Teddy Bear enjoyed working with the real thing. Knowing that he was pressing his pointed, ink-soaked needle into what had once been a part of a living creature that he could turn into an heirloom to be treasured gave him a personal thrill and stimulated his creative juices.

If Teddy Bear was going to be able to continue his business and expand his fame and the size of his pocketbook, he had to find sources that would complement those dwindling materials coming from his supplier.

By fate, luck or coincidence—it didn't matter to Teddy Bear what it was called—good fortune arrived and alleviated all of his concerns.

One fall afternoon he was exploring a nearby barrier island, off the Eastern Coast not far from his home. The site was part of a 45-mile, loosely connected series of various-sized parcels that protected the Atlantic mainland from storms and swelling seas.

He had gone on the trip to take a few photographs, collect driftwood and enjoy a quiet day by himself. It was important to hide away from the telephone calls and people who visited his studio seeking bargains and conversations. On this day, Teddy Bear needed to be alone so he could think and regroup.

He had steered his small motorboat on the sandy shoreline of Killer Cove Island, not far from Wallace Point and Straight Sandy Beach. It had been his favorite getaway spot for years, and Teddy Bear had never told a living soul about where he spent his private time. He would thank God for that decision for the rest of his life, for it was on Killer Cove Island that Teddy Bear discovered his personal treasure trove.

He wasn't seeking anything in particular, just wandering the beach and shoreline, admiring nature and trying to clear his mind for some serious planning. While walking through a thick stand of brush and pine trees, he noticed a dark brown gnarled stick. It was shaped like a cane but the length bore a twisted design that had been caused by the vine that had wrapped around and embedded itself into the stick's surface.

As he pulled the interesting piece of limb, trying to break it off from the tree, the narrow stem snapped and Teddy Bear lost his footing and was tossed backwards, landing roughly against a slightly raised mound of sand.

This site turned out to be his extra special, X-marks-the-spot lucky location. For as he tried to push himself off the sandy knoll, something sharp protruding from the mound drove into his right hand.

Turning to see the source of his pain, Teddy Bear noticed a sharp, pointed white object sticking through the sandy mound. Carefully, he brushed the sand aside, and his slow-paced search revealed a skeleton hand. Further examination uncovered a nearly complete set of human bones that had been buried at the site. With the shifting sea, forceful winds and added assistance from island animals, the grave had become disturbed and exposed.

Immediately surveying the nearby area, Teddy Bear discovered 10 other gravesites, and only the approaching darkness prevented him from locating more.

After covering up all traces of his visit—and concealing the open section of the sandy crypt—Teddy decided to visit the local library and historical society and conduct some private research.

He soon learned that most of the barrier islands were home to settlers in a number of villages. While a few of these small towns established central graveyards, most families simply buried their kin on the property, usually behind or beside the dwelling.

Teddy Bear also came across newspaper articles from the early 1800s referring to several "unknown sailors" plots. These were barren, out-of-the-way locations where bodies washed up on shore. Usually, they were placed below the sand very close to where they had been found. These sites went unattended and most were never recorded. Therefore, their exact locations cannot be determined, and anyone suggesting where they are at present is offering nothing more than a good guess.

Teddy Bear smiled when he read an official state government document stating: "All residents of the islands moved to the mainland. In a few instances, remains of immediate family members also were moved onto the mainland and reburied near the new homesteads."

But not all. Teddy Bear knew that for sure. And it didn't take the scrimshaw artist much time to realize the significance of his find.

While sitting in his parlor—sipping warm tea and delicately holding a thick portion of the skeleton finger he had brought home from the island—Teddy Bear knew the bodies had long ago been forgotten. In fact, the poor souls eventually would waste away to dust out on Killer Cove Island. He could perform a service for those discarded lonesome creatures.

Not only could Teddy Bear get them back onto the mainland, but he could deliver them directly into the modern mainstream of life—as earrings and rings, as pocket watch faces and penknife cases, as desk paperweights and tie clips. After all, jewelry was his specialty, and the appearance of small pieces of human bone wasn't that different from the working surfaces of whale teeth and ivory.

Teddy Bear grinned. There was no stopping him now. He had an unlimited supply of material, and only his imagination and drive restricted the opportunities on the horizon.

Smiling, he picked up his sharp hand file. Carefully, the scrimshaw scribe began to smooth off the rough edges of the unknown sailor's finger bone. Soon, very soon, he would deliver a very special, one-of-a-kind tie clip to Mary's Boutique by the Sea.

Author's note: To read a true story about the history and ghostly events associated with the Unknown Sailors Graveyard, located in Lewes, Delaware, beneath the Cape May-Lewes Ferry parking lot, see *Crying in the Kitchen*, Vol. VI of the *Spirits Between the Bays* Mid-Atlantic ghost/folklore series.

Superstitions and Legends

of the Beaches, Bays and Seas

Watermen are careful to avoid the use of walnut in the construction of boats. Traditionally, the wood was employed to make coffins. If walnut is used to make or repair a boat, they believe the craft is sure to experience bad luck.

Some watermen on Maryland's Eastern Shore still believe that blue is a bad luck color for a boat. Never paint blue on any part of a boat, they say. Some stories tell of fishermen turning their boats around and heading back to shore if they discover anything bearing the color blue on their boat.

The superstition associated with the color blue dates back to the days when American Indians paddled the waters of the Chesapeake Bay. Indians who lived near the Choptank River would never paint the color blue on their canoes because that color belonged to the water gods. The Indians believed if they used blue, it would make the spirit beings jealous and unhappy.

Because Christ died during His Crucifixion on a Friday, most sea captains considered it a bad-luck day to begin a journey. Therefore, many sailors preferred to leave from port on any other day of the week. Some, in fact, recalling Christ's Resurrection, preferred to embark on Sunday, the most holy day of the week.

For nearly two centuries, the "Weather Witch" would visit the Delaware Bay, stirring up a storm every time a salvage operation was close to raising the *HMS DeBraak*, which sank at Cape Henlopen near Lewes harbor on May 25, 1798. The submerged vessel was eventually raised in August 1988, and on that night the "Bad Weather Witch" made her final appearance, nearly disrupting the salvage effort. (See the complete story in *Crying in the Kitchen,* Vol. VI of the *Spirits Between the Bays* Mid-Atlantic ghost/folklore series.)

Crows are a sign of bad luck if one flies across a boat. But, if two or more happen to fly across a craft, it means there will be a good catch on that day.

The Irish believed that the banshee could not cross water. On the Delmarva Peninsula, some also claim that ghosts cannot cross water. As a result, an abundance of spirits are trapped on the 14 counties nestled between the Chesapeake and Delaware Bays. This also may account for the large number of sightings of apparitions at Fort Delaware, located on Pea Patch Island.

The following superstitions are from "Weather Oddities," which appeared in *Peninsula Pacemaker* in January 1991. They are shared by Hazel D. Brittingham, Lewes historian and author of *Lanterns on Lewes*. She also is a popular speaker and an expert on the topic of Atlantic lighthouses.

"Wind from the south has water in its mouth."
"A sunshiny shower never lasts an hour."

"Red sky at night, sailor's delight.
Red sky at morning, sailor take warning."

Slaves and their immediate descendants were particularly fearful of dolphins. They believed dolphins would call out the names of those traveling on nearby ships, and, to satisfy the cries of these sea creatures, those named would be tossed overboard as a sacrifice to the sea. Even in the early 20th century, descendants of slaves on the Eastern Shore of Maryland displayed great fear when schools of dolphins appeared.

Pirates would leave behind a crew member's dead body atop a buried treasure chest to guard the hidden loot and keep hunters from stealing the precious booty. It was believed that anyone finding treasure would be horrified when he discovered the remnants of a dead sailor. If the hunter persisted in trying to reach the treasure, he would have to dig past and handle the bones of the dead sentry. Disturbing the rotted remains of the guard would antagonize the dead body's spirit and deliver bad luck to the treasure hunter. For this list of reasons, it was believed the searcher would give up the hunt.

To insure a steady supply of wind, some captains would hire a witch or shaman to sail on the voyage. This would ensure that if the sea winds failed for too long a period of time, the magician would be on board and available to conjure up a breeze to move the vessel along.

Since the 1800s, coins with the image of King George III have been discovered on the Delaware shore immediately north of the Indian River Inlet. So many copper coins—and some made of gold and silver—were found that the area became known as Coin Beach. Some believe the coins are from the wreck of the *Faithful Steward*, which was heading to Philadelphia from Ireland but wrecked near the Sussex County shore in September 1785. The cargo included hundreds of barrels of half pennies and other coins.

Today, modern treasure hunters, armed with sophisticated metal detectors, still search this beach site and others trying to discover long hidden coins and valuables that are concealed beneath the sand and sea.

To keep ghosts out of a house, some dwellers in the Eastern Shore watertowns, and in English fishing villages as well, suggest the homeowner place a penny—with the head facing up—over the window and door, on the sills. It's also good practice to place a penny in each corner of each room in the house. This practice also has been used successfully by some to get rid of unwanted spirits.

To get an indication of a child's future, place a coin, a copy of *The Bible* and a bottle of whiskey in front of the baby. If the child touches the money first, he or she will become a banker or accountant. If it first selects *The Bible*, the child will become a minister, priest or preacher. But, if the baby grabs the bottle first, it will become a drunk.

When the sea winds died and the air was still, sailing ship mariners believed they could generate a breeze that would fill the sails by whistling. However, they had to be careful not to offer too spirited a tune, for they did not want a dangerous gale but only a steady wind that would send the wooden sailing ship along its way.

Sailors murdered at sea will not rest until their killer has been found and punished.

Cats on a boat make many old mariners edgy, for they believe the animals—an alternative lifeform of a witch—will surely bring bad luck.

In some cases, cats were taken to sea, but their activities were watched very carefully. It was believed that if the animal became agitated, disappeared or fell overboard it was a sign that a storm was approaching.

Occasionally, in historic watertowns on mainlands and on islands you can find the remnants of modest-sized bell towers standing beside gravesites. According to George Reynolds Sr., Elk Mills, Maryland, historian and archaeologist, the term "saved by the bell," did not originate during prizefights and boxing matches, nor did it refer to students who were happy to hear the signal announcing the end of a school day.

In olden times, people who feared they might pass out or become unconscious from strange diseases and be mistaken for dead requested that a rope be placed in their hands inside their coffin. The cord was attached to a bell hanging outside the gravesite. If the unfortunate person awoke in the coffin, he or she could yank on the rope and ring the bell, thereby saving themselves from being buried alive.

St. Elmo's Fire, a bright light that would appear as a result of meeting storm fronts and electricity in the atmosphere, was considered a sign of good luck by those sailing the dark seas. Often, the electrical charge would appear near the top of shipmasts and trees. Some believed it insured a safe journey, since the ship had fallen under the protection of Saint Elmo, who along with Saint Brendan, is considered a patron saint of sailors.

A blackbird on a windowsill or a bird flying in a house are sure signs of the upcoming arrival of death. Blackbirds landing on boats approaching shore is a sign that bad luck is near.

Sea serpents have been reported since the beginning of water travel, and occasionally sightings have continued into the late 20th century. Prehistoric looking water creatures have been sighted in several locales. Most famous is Scotland's Loch Ness Monster, sometimes called Nessie. Other lesser known sea monsters include Chessie of the Chesapeake Bay, Champ of Lake Champlain and Manipogo of Lake Manitoba.

Just as dwellers on the mainland reported seeing elves and fairies, werewolves and vampires, witches and ghosts, and leprechauns and angels, so too were there strange sightings at sea. Sailors, who were on the water for months at a time, would report sightings of mermaids or merfolk. These half human, half fish creatures would lure sailors into hazardous areas where their ships would be lost, or help the mariners avoid dangerous shoals that would rip the wooden ships apart.

Haunted ships have been reported throughout time. They include the *Flying Dutchman*, a vessel which disappeared but whose misty image is sighted and is considered a sure sign of bad luck to come. Others, like the *Mary Celeste*, have been discovered drifting without a crew, and speculation on the fate of the missing mariners has continued to this day. Some ships seem to have developed a haunted reputation simply because of their age and long life, such as the *USS Constellation,* located in Baltimore's Inner Harbor. Even cruise ships have stories to tell, including the *Queen Mary* ocean liner, now a tourist attraction in Long Beach, California.

Lesser known haunted vessels include pleasure craft and workboats, warships and merchant craft. They have survived turbulent storms and fierce bloody battles, only to have a significant amount of the suffering and terror they experienced remain within their hulls. From time to time, their restless resident spirits seep out and make their troubling presence known.

Sources

Brittingham, Hazel: personal interview

Clark, Jerome, *Unexplained!:* Visible Ink Press, 1993

Guthrie, Trudy: personal interview

Parry, J.H., *Romance of the Sea*:
The National Geographic Society, 1981

Reynolds, George: personal interview

A Spiritual Connection

In the North Atlantic Ocean

On March 26, 1951, three days before Easter Sunday, 21-year-old Carl Ercole was drafted into the U.S. Army, to serve in the Korean War.

After passing his physical examination in Philadelphia, Carl was placed on a bus bound for orientation at Fort Meade, Maryland. Ironically, as the bus passed through Wilmington, Delaware, it went right past his home. Already feeling homesick, he wanted to jump off the bus and return to his home, but continued on.

Being forced to leave his family and friends made Carl feel sick, but he accepted the fact that he must do his duty by entering the service and serving his country.

He was sent to Camp Pickett, Virginia, and was assigned to the Army Security Agency. After graduation from radio school in Camp Gordon, Georgia, the members of his class were given the opportunity to take part in a bizarre plan—by drawing straws—to determine their next assignment. Those who selected a small straw would go to Korea. Those who drew the long straw would end up in Germany.

It was Carl's lucky day, and he felt relieved when he pulled a long straw and knew he was headed for duty in Europe.

Carl spent his two years of military service in Germany, and on Feb. 18, 1953, he was glad to be heading back home on the *USS Butler*. The double-stacked. 1,000-foot-long ship was an awesome sight, painted dull Navy gray with five decks. The ship's lowest level was crammed with sleeping quarters for troops bound for home.

Halfway across the Atlantic Ocean, the ship developed a cracked bow, and incoming water had to be pumped out continuously. The thought of the huge battleship filling up with heavy sea water and slowly sinking to the bottom of the enormous ocean was terrifying. Carl and countless other soldiers prayed that they would make it home.

Getting caught in a fierce storm added to the ship's problems. Heavy winds, high seas and devastating, 60-foot waves pounded against the *Butler's* sides. For Carl, witnessing the anger and might of the furious ocean would never be forgotten, and he called upon God for protection through the difficult times.

During most of the trip home, Carl was seasick and suffered with a temperature that reached 102 degrees. He continually stood with his head bent over the deck garbage cans, vomiting up green fragments of nothing from his empty stomach. He recalled that it felt like he had swallowed a pack of razor blades.

Only the thought of returning home kept him sane, but he realized he was at the total mercy of the powerful ocean that continued to smash against the ship's weakened hull.

Being a conscientious soldier, Carl did not complain nor make excuses when he was ordered to report to guard duty on the ship's main deck. He was assigned to the midnight to 2 a.m. shift, and when he arrived for duty, severe winds and mountain-sized waves were pounding the upper decks.

Carl's job was to walk the perimeter of the ship in the dead of night, all alone. No one else was on deck except a naval officer, but he manned the lookout tower, which was higher up and located toward the *Butler's* bow.

Carl described that experience as a "night full of terror and anxiety." The smell and taste of death lurked at every turn. The mighty roar of the huge waves and strong gusting winds paralyzed his mind. Suddenly, without warning, a rolling wave rushed over the top of the ship, smashing Carl with such tremendous force that it swept him off his feet and knocked him face down onto the steel deck.

In his sick and weakened condition, Carl knew he had no strength to keep himself from being washed across the slippery deck and swept overboard into the black water.

As his body slid atop the metal surface, his right shoulder smashed against a metal railing. Frantically, he grabbed onto the slippery bar and wrapped his arms around it in a desperate death-lock to keep from being swept overboard. Too weak to scream and too terrified to move, Carl knew that in the howling wind, no one would have heard his cries for help.

Carl closed his eyes. In a state of agonizing fear, he used all his strength to hold tight to the railing. And for what seemed an eternity, he prayed he would be saved before the ocean pulled him off the ship.

It was only when he saw his replacement appear to take over the watch that Carl was able to loosen his deathgrip and move slowly and carefully off the hazardous deck.

When he was safely in the bowels of the rolling ship, a shaking Carl decided he would never mention the incident to a living soul. It was an experience he said he would rather forget. He also knew he had never had the strength to hold on against the more powerful ocean. He was sure that God and His goodness had intervened and saved him from drowning at sea.

Days later, the *Butler* arrived in New York harbor. Within a few weeks, Carl returned home and was thankful to be safe and secure among family and friends.

It was late in the afternoon on the day of his arrival, when Carl remarked that he had not seen his older brother, Lewis, who was the most religious member of the family and who often kept to himself more than the others.

Carl excused himself from the group and went to visit Lew in the older man's room, where they sat and talked for quite a while. As Carl got up to leave and return to the rest of the family, Lew said, "You know, Carl, I had a terrible dream about you, and it woke me up out of a sound sleep. I dreamed that you were drowning."

Lewis added that his dream was so real that he jotted down the date and time that it had occurred. To the brothers' mutual surprise, the dream took place at the exact time and date that Carl had been hit by the gigantic wave while on watch duty. At the same time Lew saw the scene

in his dream, Carl was holding onto the railing of the storm-tossed ship.

Stunned and speechless, Carl left the room shaken.

A month had passed since the terrifying incident in the Atlantic Ocean, and Carl had never mentioned it to anyone. He had made an effort to bury the memory.

To think that at the very moment in time, when Carl was on the verge of being swallowed into the sea thousands of miles away, in his home, his brother was dreaming that Carl was drowning.

The dream was so real, Lewis said, that he woke up with a heavy heart and asked God to watch over his younger brother.

Was it fate?

Was it mental telepathy?

Or was it a spiritual connection between two brothers?

Does anyone really know the answer?

Carl said he believes God laid his hand on him that night in the middle of the vast, stormy Atlantic Ocean. Perhaps the Almighty was alerted to Carl's needs through the prayers of his brother, who was a continent away, in Wilmington, Delaware.

—Andy Ercole

Editor's note: This true story was provided by Delaware resident Andy Ercole, a talented author and a good friend. I had the pleasure to work with Andy when we co-authored the biography *Tiberi: The Uncrowned Champion* in 1992. More recently, Andy's latest book, *Don't Walk In My Shoes,* was released in December 2000. For information on this very interesting biography of Barbara Anne Blaze, contact Andy Ercole by mail at RR-5 Box 230, Harbeson, DE 19951.

A Horrifyingly True Fishing Story

Wilmington and Lewes, Delaware

I grew up in the city, close to factories and freight yards, gin mills and street lights. While the kids from the suburbs spent the summer at the shore, we played in the front yard (a narrow, ribbon-shaped concrete sidewalk) or the backyard (a larger, square-shaped concrete sidewalk).

Now, don't get me wrong; I'm not complaining. After all, pitching pennies, a game of dodge ball or dropping a nickel in the Linden Grille pinball were fine with me. But after I was married and had children, things seemed to change.

Like most parents, I tried to give my kids opportunities and experiences that I hadn't had. When my older son, Eddie, was 7, he begged me to take him fishing.

"Please?" he cried. "All the other kids' fathers do. Come on, Dad; I really want to go."

The water welled up in his eyes, the heartbreaking frown dropped toward the floor and a genuine, honest-to-God tear rolled down his cheek, landing on the back of my hand.

What's a father to do?

I changed the subject, tossed him in the car and went out and got him a pizza.

That had worked in the past and, for a few more weeks, the art of bribery with junk food weaved its magic again. But, eventually, my son reappeared, reciting the same plea, offering the same rationale and comparing me again to the wonderful fathers who did anything their kids wanted.

Again the water welled up in his eyes, like before the heart-breaking frown dropped toward the floor and, this time, three tears landed on the back of my hand.

This time I did the only thing possible: I stupidly said "Yes." But since I didn't know a hook from a reel or a fly from a rod, I called upon my old friend Sambo, expert fisherman of the rivers, ponds, bays and oceans, for assistance.

For years, Sambo had been trying to get me out in the bay, "to do a little deep sea," but I had adamantly refused.

"No way! I don't go anywhere the water is above my head, unless I'm on a bridge. Plus," I added, "I don't like wasting my whole day sitting in the sun, drinking warm beer and cleaning slimy creatures that I can buy at the corner market where they're already wrapped in cellophane and ready to throw in the pan."

But after putting up a valiant battle for years, my son made me hoist the flag of surrender. At 3 a.m. on a Saturday, when everyone with any sense was sound asleep, we loaded up Sambo's Bronco with coolers, nets, bait and ice.

"Don't forget the ice," he reminded me 20 times. "We'll need to pack down our catch. Don't want the boatload to spoil on the way home," he explained, flashing me a confident smile.

U.S. 13 wasn't as deserted as I'd expected, because our headlights spotted a number of other crazies, pulling their boats and trailers toward the waiting sand and surf.

Sambo assured me, however, that our spot was on a secluded island off Lewes, which we would have to ourselves and "catch the big ones until our arms fall off."

Although Sambo was totally sincere, and my son's face beamed with innocent excitement, I couldn't get rid of the nagging feeling that the trip was destined to be a disaster.

En route, we made a "pit stop," as Sambo described it, at the Kirby and Halloway Family Restaurant in Dover. After a big breakfast of scrapple, eggs and hash browns, we continued south and arrived at the Roosevelt Inlet, just north of the sleepy town of Lewes.

One of Sambo's friends was waiting with a small boat, got us aboard and deposited us on the tip of a spit of sand at 7 a.m. He promised to pick us up at 5 in the afternoon, giving us 10 hours of fun, solitude and relaxation. By 10 minutes past 7, my son had his line in the water, and by 7:15 he was asking why he hadn't had a bite.

Sambo just laughed, leaned back in his special metal beach chair (which didn't have any legs), lowered his floppy "lucky fishing hat" over his eyes and went to sleep.

I, on the other hand, was busy watching my son, baiting his line and dodging the hook, which he tossed haphazardly each time he tried to cast.

At noon, five hours after arrival and when neither of the two men of the sea had felt so much as a tug on his line, we opened the cooler for lunch. Behind the backdrop of my companion's uproarious laughter, I retrieved our soggy sandwiches and mushy potato chips, which were floating in the melted ice.

The sun was hot, my throat was dry, my stomach was growling and my kid was moaning about not catching any fish. Other than that, everything was perfect. What a great way to spend my day off. And only five more hours to go . . . .

It was 2 p.m. when disaster struck.

I was hunched over the cooler, staring at the damp slices of bread, which were attracting flies and other strange sand insects and creatures that I never knew existed. As I looked up at my son, standing 20 feet away, he cocked his rod in preparation for throwing his line into the sea. Suddenly, I thought, *I hope doesn't hook anybody with that thing.*

Then, like a slow-motion movie, I saw him yank the rod forward. It didn't respond, and I wondered what he could have snagged.

When he tugged a second time, I saw a slight flash of moving line, heading in my direction and, simultaneously, I felt my right ear move. Immediately, he gave two more quick, rough jerks, and my ear, after the briefest interval, seemed to be on fire.

"YOU HOOKED ME!" I screamed, as I flew off the cooler. "THE DAMN KID'S *PULLING OFF MY EAR!*"

I didn't even try to maintain control.

The miserable, stupid day. The intense heat. No lunch. No stupid fish. No sleep. I had hated it all from the beginning. Now, to top it off, my kid had put a hole in my body. That was the limit.

After listening to a dozen "I'm sorries" from my son and a fair number of "You've got big problems, pal," from Sambo, I decided that my two companions were three degrees below useless.

Holding an ice cube against my wound and sporting the latest in fish hook jewelry—complete with six inches of wet line—I ran to the shore and signaled for assistance from a passing boat.

Using a pair of wire cutters, my rescuer clipped off the hook, shoved the metal stem through my earlobe, bandaged my wound and gave us a ride back to the mainland.

We returned to the civilization of the city without a load of fish and minus a portion of my right ear.

Curled up in the rear of the Bronco, I pretended to be asleep and listened to Sambo and my son agreeing with each other about the big ones that got away. And I groaned quietly, because I realized that was how fishermen, and monsters, were born.

Author's note: This event occurred in 1978 at Roosevelt Inlet, off Lewes, Delaware. The author has not been on a fishing trip since. Little Eddie is now 30 years old and an accomplished fisherman. My friend Sambo continues to prowl the Delaware Bay and Atlantic Ocean in search of the "Big One."

'Did Ya See a Puffin?'

Northern Maine and North Atlantic Ocean

I've never fared well on boats—or ships, either. In fact, things that move and I don't seem to get along with each other very well.

I can recall quite clearly becoming ill when I was a kid, riding in the back of the car during family trips in the 1950s. Many years later, after I'd mastered my adverse reactions to motion in automobiles, I got seasick crossing the Delaware Bay on one of the huge, slow moving ships of the Cape May-Lewes Ferry fleet.

I refuse to fly on airplanes, especially after a friend of mine with a private pilot license took me up in a compact four-seater. Even before he did a few loops and engine stalls—making the plane drop in midair "just for fun," as he said—I had filled up two plastic bags with whatever had been resting in my stomach.

I also tried trains. Most of the time, the rails and I were a compatible couple, except on that lengthy trip from Washington, D.C., to Chicago, when I got sick the first night in my sleeping compartment.

With such a history, I'll never understand how I got myself into the absolutely worst "seasick" situation of my life. In fact, as I think back on my "boat trip from hell," I truly believe it's a miracle that I'm alive and able to share the story.

I read *The Perfect Storm*, and I've seen the horrifying movie scene on the video box cover of the tiny ship amidst a colossal wave. Now, I'm not claiming that I was on the high seas in a situation equally bad. But, according to my very clear recollection, during a terrifying summer day in the stormy North Atlantic Ocean I knew I was going to perish and, as the hours wore on, I actually was looking forward to it.

Let me explain.

I hate to travel. Let me drive my car for a full day up and down the Delmarva Peninsula, interviewing interesting people and I am a happy man. I get to see familiar sights, get away from it all, pick up fascinating stories and tales and, return to my home, family and dogs and then retire to my familiar bed. To me, such a life is grand.

Make me go on a trip that lasts more than overnight and I become irritable, miserable and an A-1 complainer who can't wait to get back home. I don't like strolling through gift shops, visiting museums, examining antiques, taking pictures or being trapped in groups forced to listen to tour guides. I would rather be off on my own and making practical use of my time.

Plus, since I won't fly—and my wife won't fly or take the train, if we decide to go anywhere our only mode of transportation is driving. Which I enjoy—except if its in heavy traffic.

Obviously, we don't go away very often. And when we do, it's memorable . . . and disastrous.

Our summer trip to Maine was no exception. In fact, it was the worst experience of my adult life.

So much for background, now let me focus on the essence of the story.

Knowing my aversion to leaving home, my wife, Kathleen, decided that she would need a ploy to convince me to accompany her on a 10-day trip to Maine. For some reason, she loves the state and enjoys going there to explore beautiful sites so she can capture them in her watercolor paintings.

I wasn't receptive, and I'm sure I declined immediately.

But, as any married man knows, women have a way of nudging and pecking and wearing you down like you were the victim of Chinese water torture.

One night, about a week after she had first raised the trip idea, she showed me an article in a glossy travel magazine about Captain Horace. The old salt takes people, for a $50 fee each, 20 miles out into the North Atlantic. His destination is a private island, complete with lighthouse, where he guides his ship's passengers to sites where they can photograph puffins.

"What in the world are puffins?" I wondered.

"These sweet little birds," Kath said, pointing to a full-color picture of what looked like midget penguins with red and yellow heads. "Aren't they cute? Wouldn't you like to see some?"

I answered, "No and no!"

Then she uttered her preplanned suggestion, tossed me the bone that she knew I would bite on hard. "Oh. That's a shame. I just thought that while we were on the sea captain's boat you could take pictures and interview him. I'm sure he's very colorful. Then you could put his interesting story in one of your books."

"How old's this guy?" I asked.

"82."

"And how long's he been doing this?"

Smiling, she passed me the magazine and added, "Why don't you read the article."

I did, and the next day she said she had been able to confirm boat reservations that I'm sure, although I have no proof, she had made a week before. She even announced proudly that she had spoken directly with the famous Captain Horace and he would be willing to talk to me for my story.

That's not his real name, of course. But, I'll not reveal his true identity, since he might still be alive (although I hope that's not the case, and I hope his crazy 60-year-old son also is floating in the deepest corner of Davy Jone's Locker).

As I had predicted, the trip heading north was a fiasco. We left at 4 in the morning, calculated perfectly, it seemed to me, to get us stuck in rush hour and/or construction traffic on the Garden State Parkway in New Jersey. We also hit back-ups as we became tangled up in highway work while attempting to avoid New York City, and crawled along on inadequate roads approaching the Tappan Zee Bridge across the Hudson River. We also hit snarls on turnpikes in both Connecticut and Massachusetts.

What a fun way to spend the first day.

At some point we arrived in Maine. And then we drove, and drove and drove a bit more. Up we went, along the coast, through little scenic towns and past small harbors that used to host fishing fleets. But those days are long gone. Today, these town ports have become pleasure boat basins for gleaming white fiberglass boats that cost more than most people's houses.

It was the most horrible trip of my life.

"Having a good time?" Kath asked.

"Great!" I said, "just one damn beautiful boring scene after another."

Things were not going well.

After two miserable days, we arrived at the Blueberry Basket Motel. (They love blueberries up there. Everybody grows them and eats them.) We were staying along the state's northern coastline. The only thing that impressed me was the miserable state's monstrous size. I mean, I could have driven through six other more normal-sized, East coast colonies in the time we had spent traveling northward in Maine alone.

No one state should have that much land. But since it all looks alike, there's a good chance we were just riding around in circles. Also, I decided there is only a handful of people who actually live in Maine—the rest are out-of-state tourists looking for fishing towns that died out 120 years ago. There also are quite a few storekeepers, who have moved up from New York and New Jersey.

You can drive for 100 miles and not see a house or a person, and that was the only enjoyable part of the trip.

But, back to the impending horror.

As we checked into the Blueberry Basket, my wife mentioned we were going to go out with Captain Horace the next morning.

"Gonna see ya some puffins, eh?" the motel guy said, then his face telegraphed a concerned look, and he added, "You ain't heading out tomorra, are ya. Say a storm's comin'." Then he jutted his chin toward the door, and we turned and looked at the cloudy sky.

Smiling, my wife replied, "We're supposed to call the captain tonight and check in. He'll let us know, but I'm sure it will be fine."

Blueberry Man shrugged his shoulders, gave us the room key and provided directions to the town's sole restaurant and a Rite Aide Pharmacy, both of which would close promptly at 8 p.m., and he wished us a good night's rest.

We were scheduled to stay there three days. The Basket would serve as our outpost for explorations into nearby Canada, along the rocky coasts and wherever else we happened to wind up.

After a quick supper, Kath's call to Captain Horace confirmed it was a go for the following morning.

"He said we're set," she told me, placing down the phone following a brief conversation with our hired maritime guide. "He said not to worry about the weather. He's been doing this for more than 60 years, and he can tell when things will be rough. And this trip won't."

Exhausted from the long drive up, I shut off the light, pretended I was home in my own bed and, trying to be positive, reviewed the questions I would ask Captain Horace during the interview on his boat.

The sky was a dull gray shroud when we arrived at the Shipsport Dock. There wasn't much activity stirring, and I wasn't surprised. Surely, the trip would be a bust, we would get back our $100 and I could convince my wife it was time to pack up, end the vacation and head for home.

No such luck.

A half dozen birds-and-bunnies, environmental wacko types were seated along the deck of our vessel—aptly named *Puffin III*—as we stepped down from the damp pier and boarded the weathered craft.

As we had approached from the parking lot, I thought I had seen Captain Horace's ship before—in the movie *Jaws.* It resembled the floating bucket of unpainted boards and rocking motion that had been commanded by a nasty fellow named Quint. This boat had to be the sister ship of that one which sank near the end of the movie.

Beside the self-appointed Friends of the Earth—who were wearing yellow rain slickers, skull caps and puffy Arctic-weather-style gloves—rested a half-dozen stainless steel chests, plus canvas bags and assorted camping equipment. We soon learned that our captain and his son had agreed to deposit the scraggly assortment of researchers on the island and return to pick them up the following week.

In effect, the enterprising seaman was double dipping on the trip—taking a bunch of puffin people out for pictures plus making a taxi run to the island as well.

There were about 20 stupid souls on *Puffin III*, in addition to our two mariner hosts. The paid sightseers came from as far away as Illinois and Tennessee. Obviously, Captain Horace's fame had spread some distance.

Each passenger was well prepared for the day, armed with a camera—several owners had expensive models with telescopic sights—a lunch bag, drinks and heavy clothing to keep the water and wind at bay.

Amid introductions and a few quips and bursts of laughter—most of it designed to calm individual concerns about the weather—Captain and Son cast off toward the open sea. But first we had to exit the calm, gray harbor, which was enclosed by a 20-foot-tall rusted metal sea wall that extended from and connected two shorelines about a half-mile apart. This made it impossible for us to see the condition of the Atlantic Ocean, until we had passed that morning's point of no return.

Too stupid to question our host's decision making, and obviously ignorant of nautical weather conditions, all of us paying customers acted as if we were having a wonderful time. We did this in spite of the fact that immediately upon entering the open sea the old wooden boat began to buck like a bronco. It was only 10 minutes later, when I looked back and realized that the sea wall was too far behind for even an accomplished swimmer to reach. That also was the moment when the lurching and dropping of the boat, as its hull repeatedly slammed against the gray green water, reminded me of the roller coaster rides that I never, ever enjoyed—and sensibly avoided.

About the same moment, I noticed that no one was talking. Small talk and smiles had been left behind at the dock. Everyone was holding quite tightly onto whatever was near—be it a pipe, section of a seat or hunk of deck—and shifting their eyes rapidly from person to person. No doubt each sane person was trying to determine if anyone else indeed thought that what was occurring might be abnormal.

The schedule was for us to leave dock at 7 a.m., head out across the great deep to the island and be transported during the last leg of the journey by a rowboat at about 10 a.m. After spending an hour searching for and snapping shots of puffins, we would reboard our ocean craft and head for the mainland, arriving back in Shipsport about 2 in the afternoon.

It was 7:20 a.m., less than one-half hour into the seven-hour-pleasure trip, when I bolted out of the cabin, shoved my head over the side and tossed whatever was traveling through my throat and mouth into the swelling Atlantic.

With my stomach twisted, my body soaked and chills beginning to make their presence known, I was very certain that it was going to be a long bad day.

I was wrong. It was going to turn catastrophic.

It didn't matter to me that I was alone heaving up my innards over the side. And I didn't care what anyone thought of me. I would never see these idiots again. Between churns of my stomach, I realized that this was only the start, and that the pain and discomfort would continue for the next six-and-a-half hours (or 390 minutes). Count the moments of pain anyway you like, it still comes out to an unbearable amount of time.

Worst of all, I also knew there was no way the captain would shorten the trip.

At 8:15 a.m., when I was seated alone in the rear of the boat, underneath an overhang from the little cabin where all the rest of my frightened shipmates were huddled, I noticed sheets of water were cascading down upon me, soaking my coat, clothing, camera, tape recorder and skin. And I didn't care one damn bit, because I couldn't move.

Movement of any sort—in fact, just thinking about it—might cause my stomach demons to reawaken. I estimated that I had been sitting in an uncomfortable upright position for 15 minutes, and there was no way anyone or anything was going to make me move. Besides, no one would come near me anyway. I was treated like a wet leper. All of my other wretched shipmates were afraid if they even looked in my direction, let alone got near me, my seasickness would leap from my body and attach itself to them. For their salvation, they let me be—and for that I was grateful.

At that moment, and for the rest of the overpriced tour, I hated everyone—that included my wife, the ancient captain and his stupid elderly son, the Earth loving, tree hugging researchers as well as all the other fare paying idiots who had kept quiet as we entered the stormy sea.

Around 9 a.m., the waves were reaching well beyond the sides of the boat. That also wasn't a good sign, but no one else complained, so I suffered in silence. Looking out to the rolling, threatening sea, I noticed that when the waves receded for a few moments, I had an opportunity to look out into the distance, and I saw islands that stood off the coastline.

I heard a male tourist in a designer jacket urge that the boat move in closer, so he could take some pictures of the area's natural unspoiled beauty. As *Puffin III* changed course and headed toward the narrow spit of land, I hoped we would strike rock, yearned to hear the sound of the boat's wooden hull being ripped to shreds. Then, we would have to dive overboard and wait to be rescued on the surface of a beach that didn't rock.

But good fortune was not to be. Things again got worse.

Responding to another dimwitted paying customer's request to remain on site a few moments to get more artistic photographs, Captain Horace killed the motor. That stopped our forward motion, but it didn't halt our sideways movement. That rocking intensified, compliments of the turbulent forces of the ocean.

At that moment, I recall thinking that it felt like someone had tied me into a soaking cloth hammock, while I was out in a downpour gagging from nausea, and then I was being rolled and rocked back and forth, up and down, sideways and backwards, with a force that I knew would never end.

To get through that miserable moment, my right hand was gripped tightly around a cold metal bar. I was holding on, trying to relieve my upper body's pressure from jamming into my stomach. Suddenly, the boat began to rock violently. Packages and bags, metal chests and fire extinguishers, clothing and cameras began rolling across the deck. People began losing their footing and several of my mates raced to find a seat or claim a portion of the craft to lean against or cling to.

Again, I leaned over at my special shipside spot to deposit more of my stomach contents into the sea.

If I had retained any amount of strength I might have considered shouting out, "Are you people NUTS? We're going to go under unless we turn back NOW!" But I just kept quiet. Probably because the pain was so bad and I had told God that I really wanted to die. And, if given the chance, I would have been happy to take the rest of the idiots with me.

Someone passed the word that we would be at the island in about two hours. "Isn't that great?" a smiling woman told me. I couldn't answer and just waved a weak hand.

Laughing caught my attention next. As I looked up, I noticed Son of the Evil Captain Horace was pointing to me and shouting, "Ain't no way he's gonna have a good time!"

Dad nodded his wrinkled turkey face, agreeing with his clever offspring and tossed out an agreeing laugh.

I hated them both. Hated the old fossil of a father and loathed their stupid Maine accents.

I also despised my wife, God and the person and crew that had constructed *Puffin III.* I hated the concrete team who worked on the Maine highways that got us there, the Blueberry motel man who let us stay overnight and the guys in the GM factory that had built my car.

I was ready to dive over the side. But I couldn't stand up. So I closed my eyes, but that didn't help, I just got dizzier. I had to keep them open and record every horribly painful moment, and I promised that someone was going to pay.

When you're deathly seasick, no amount of deep breathing helps. Nor does it matter if use your mouth or nose, if you take short breaths or long ones, or if you close your eyes or keep them open. Your entire body is a toxic timebomb, trapped in a hellish holding pattern from which there is no quick escape—except drowning. And, that can become a serious option.

Eventually, our battered craft made it to the area near the island. Son of Captain Horace loaded the research gang into a rowboat and deposited them on the rocky shore, near the lighthouse. But when he came back, he announced that the sea was too rough and he couldn't risk dropping us off to search for puffins.

"I just about made it back, myself," the seaman stated. Then added that *Puffin III* would circle the island a few times and give the birders opportunities to shoot pictures from the slow moving, rocking boat.

The good news that we wouldn't be roaming the island for a few hours had put us ahead of schedule. The bad news was that each time the boat stopped for a picture taking session, the horrible side-to-side rocking motion would begin again. And that made my seasickness worse.

A voice in my mind told me not to look at my watch. I would only become disappointed. But I couldn't help it. I was tired of staring straight ahead, so I peeked at the soaked Timex. It had stopped sometime around 10:47 a.m. I guessed that it had to be close to noon.

For another 20 minutes or so, I hung over the side of the rocking vessel. In the background, I heard the Captain announce we were heading back in, to the mainland. I was gleeful, almost ready to respond with applause like a little child. Then one of the birder idiots shouted back, "Can we please have another 20 minutes?"

As the captain reluctantly agreed to the request, I wanted to crawl across the deck like a water soaked spider, grab the picture-taking cretin's leg, drag him to the floor and beat the living crap out of the idiot.

But instead I threw up, which is what I did best.

A half hour later, as *Puffin III* was moving swiftly toward shore, which was nowhere to be seen, I noticed I had been joined by a few more paying passengers. They had appeared as I was looking down into the drink. Each of them had staked out a portion of the rear deck and, to varying degrees of seriousness, hung over the side and tossed some of their breakfast or lunch out as fish food. One or two were howlers, the other three were quiet moaners. At least, at that point in time.

A spirited conversation was developing inside the cabin. I heard Son of Captain Horace arguing with the older seaman about whether this, or one other time, was the roughest sea on which they had ever sailed.

They seemed totally unconcerned about making it into port safely. But I was beginning to worry. I didn't know if it was due to five hours of retching and being soaked to the skin, or maybe it was because of the cold water chills or lack of food. But I was sure that the trip back was rougher than the first half of the voyage.

Not that my opinion counted, and not that I was able to share the thought with anyone. I was still the worst looking paying passenger on the craft. Later, my wife, who had stayed in the cabin the entire time, said she would occasionally ask someone who would come in from the rear deck if her husband was still on board.

I think the reason she didn't come out and see for herself was a genuine fear of finding me alive and of being afraid that I would strangle her and toss her lovely warm corpse overboard.

I was too weak to do either, but in my water-soaked mind those precise satisfying scenes were played out more than a few times.

Suddenly, I felt a smile form. I spotted the islands, the ones that were about two hours out from shore. I recalled our slow passage near them on the way out, and I prayed no one would ask to visit them now.

Unfortunately, one birder did, but Son of the Captain said it was getting too rough and we had to keep heading in. That was good news in one way, since we wouldn't waste any more time at sea. The bad news, in my mind, was that the ocean must really be treacherous. I wondered if we could last two more hours.

Exhausted, wet and tired of praying, I fell asleep. I'm still amazed that it was possible, but after all those hours of tension and cold, I guess my body simply shut down. The next thing I knew, we were approaching the dock. *Puffin III* had landed. Praise the Lord and pass the ammunition, for I had about six people I wanted to kill.

My wife appeared, walked toward me, grabbed my arm and raised me into a standing position. We headed off, hand in hand, not because I was in a caring, appreciative mood, but because I couldn't walk without assistance.

Captain Horace stood near the plank, mumbling something to each customer as we departed. I tried to avoid him, but he didn't pick up the deadly vibes radiating off my tense body. All I wanted was to be ignored.

Looking right into my eyes, he walked over, paused and shouted, "Did ya see a puffin?"

I tried to move my saturated right fist toward his neck, but my wife held it down with both her hands. I didn't respond, but she, ever the diplomat, actually thanked the marine maniac for the terror ride. If I had any reserve strength that I could summon, I would have pushed the two of them into the drink and dropped my ruined camera and tape recorder on their heads. Hell! I wanted a damn refund, and Kath was thanking the fossil for a seven-hour death ride through Water Hell!

Like a feeble patient in the assisted living wing of a nursing home, I clutched her arm that was leading me away from *Puffin III* and further up the old wooden dock. But if I couldn't kill I could still seethe. And seethe I did. It was my right.

Water dripped behind us and the others as we staggered through the parking lot, heading to another moving vehicle. For an instant, the thought of getting into anything that would move was frightening. But my American-made, metal land chariot was the quickest means of escape from Shipsport, and I was going to use it—soaked or not, sick or not, nearly dead or not.

There was no conversation in the car on the way to Blueberry Basket. All I wanted to do was get out of my wetsuit and crawl into a warm bed. It was 3 p.m. It had been an unforgettable day.

As we parked in front of our motel room, my wife got out of the passenger seat, looked at me and smiled. "Well, that was something, wasn't it?"

I didn't reply. I maintained my composure, held back from jumping across the car hood and wrapping my hands around her throat. I was too weak to talk, but I thought that type of sign language would relay my feeling appropriately.

But I held back, turned and stumbled toward the door,

"Well," she said, cheerily, "we've only got two hours and then we have reservations at "Captain Horace's Family Kitchen." Tonight's special is homemade chowder and all the shrimp and lobster you can eat. His wife makes it fresh every day. So we'll have to get dressed soon. Nothing fancy. We can wear casual clothes. Okay?"

I stood at the doorway, grinned like Jack Nicholson, the way he looked in the snowbound haunted hotel during the last days of *The Shining*. Then I walked in our room, took a very hot shower and went to bed.

We never made it to the Horace Family dinner event. We never made another stop in the wretched state of Maine. We rose before the sun, at dark o'clock, and headed for home. I drove 13 hours straight through, with one rest stop in North Jersey.

The neighbors were surprised to see us. They were supposed to watch the dogs for 10 days, we were back in less than four.

Actually, there were times in the North Atlantic when I thought they were going to be watching our dogs forever.

It was a silent ride home. To maintain our safety and in an attempt to salvage our marriage, neither of us initiated any conversation. I listened to the radio. My wife stared out the window, no doubt vowing never to arrange a vacation with me again.

From my perspective, that was fine.

"I hate to travel. Let me drive my car for a full day up and down the Delmarva Peninsula, interviewing interesting people and I am a happy man. I get to see familiar sights, get away from it all, pick up fascinating stories and tales and, return to my home, family and dogs and then retire to my familiar bed. To me, such a life is grand.

"Like I always told her, 'Make me go on a trip that lasts more than overnight and I become irritable, miserable and an A-1 complainer who can't wait to get back home.' "

Ed and Kathleen Okonowicz

Photo by Bob Cohen

Ed Okonowicz, a Delaware native, is an editor and writer at the University of Delaware, where he also teaches both storytelling and feature writing classes. Kathleen Burgoon Okonowicz, a watercolor artist and illustrator, is originally from Greenbelt, Maryland, and is an artist member of the Baltimore Watercolor Society.

A professional storyteller, Ed presents programs throughout the Mid-Atlantic region. He is a member of the Delaware Humanities Forum Speakers Bureau and Visiting Scholars Program and has served on the Maryland State Arts Council Traditional/Folk Arts Advisory Panel.

Kathleen enjoys taking things of the past and preserving them in her paintings. Her print, *Special Places*, features the stately stairway in Wilmington, Delaware, that was the "special place" of the characters in Ed's love story, *Stairway over the Brandywine*. In the fall of 1999, she released *Station No. 5,* a print that captures the charm of a 1893 Victorian-style firehouse also in Wilmington, near Trolley Square.

A graduate of Salisbury State University, Kathleen earned her master's degree in professional writing from Towson State University. In addition to painting, she teaches a self-publishing course at the University of Delaware.

As the owners of Myst and Lace Publishers Inc., Kathleen is responsible for art, photography, layout and design, while Ed conducts the interviews and writes the stories.

For information on storytelling, call Ed. For self-publishing or graphic design assistance, call Kathleen.
Telephone: 410 398-5013.

The sharks are gone but the ghosts never left!

128 pages
5 1/2" x 8 1/2"
softcover
ISBN 1-890690-06-6
$9.95

In *Terrifying Tales of the Beaches and Bays* and the sequel, *Terrifying Tales 2 of the Beaches and Bays*, award-winning author and storyteller Ed Okonowicz shares eerie accounts of spirits that roam the shore.

In *Terrifying Tales* 2 read about:

- Horrifying encounter in New Jersey at Graveyard Gut,
- Fort Delaware's haunted antiques and the "Door to Nowhere,"
- Sightings, orbs, cold spots and legends at Maryland's Historic Elk Landing,
- A haunted lightship, spooky fishing boat and "Little Man" in a home on The Strand,
- "Molly on the Dunes," and hauntings near the Indian River Life Saving Station
- Strange source of eerie sounds in a small town post office,
- Unspeakable problems in a million-dollar oceanfront home,
- The Eastern Shore legend of Bigg Lizz, Guardian of the Gold

and more . . . are featured in these two beach reading best sellers.

128 pages
5 1/2" x 8 1/2"
softcover
ISBN 1-890690-10-4
$9.95

Visit our web site at: www.mystandlace.com

Ghosts

Nearly 40% of Americans believe in ghosts.

Find out why, in this collection of true tales and eerie fiction, featuring

- Five college football players who fled their ghost infested apartment,
- A troubled beach home in Lewes, Delaware, and a very strange house near the C & D Canal,
- A haunted cottage near Hancock Bridge, site of a New Jersey Revolutionary War massacre,
- A haunted supermarket, ghost dog, phantom military car, eerie barn and the Pig Woman legend,
- The tale of Colonial-era Chief Justic Samuel Chew, who would not rest until he was buried—twice,
- Pesky phantoms at a Georgia Plantation Cotton Field, in a story by Jaime Cherundolo

. . . and a lot more.

Ghosts

Ed Okonowicz

112 pages
5 1/2" x 8 1/2"
softcover
ISBN 0-890690-08-2

$9.95

National Federation of Press Women First Place Award
2003

**Turn the page for a complete listing of all our books.
To order any of the titles listed, use the form on page 122.**
Books are also available at chain and local bookstores, through Amazon.com, or from our web site

The Original . . .

"If you're looking for an unusual gift for a collector of antiques, or enjoy haunting tales, this one's for you."
—Collector Editions

"This book is certainly entertaining, and it's even a bit disturbing."
—Antique Week

". . . an intriguing read."
—Maine Antique Digest

Delaware Press Association
Second Place Award
1997

A BUMP. A THUD. MYSTERIOUS MOVEMENT.

Unexplained happenings. Caused by what? Venture through this collection of short stories and discover the answer. Experience 20 eerie, true tales about items from across the country that apparently have taken on an independent spirit of their own—for they refuse to give up the ghost.

From Maine to Florida, from Pennsylvania to Wisconsin . . . haunted heirlooms exist among us . . . everywhere.

Read about them in *Possessed Possessions*, the book some antique dealers ***definitely*** do not want you to buy.

$9.95

112 pages
5 1/2" x 8 1/2"
softcover
ISBN 0-9643244-5-8

 Visit our web site at: www.mystandlace.com

and the Sequel

ACROSS THE ENTIRE COUNTRY,
POSSESSED POSSESSIONS
CONTINUE TO APPEAR.

Read about 40 more amazing true tales of bizarre, unusual and unexplained incidents—all caused by haunted objects like:

demented dolls
spirited sculptures
a pesky piano
a killer crib
and much, much more

112 pages
5 1/2" x 8 1/2"
softcover
ISBN 0-890690-02-3

$9.95

WARNING

There could be more than just dust hovering around some of the items in your home.

Visit our web site at: www.mystandlace.com

Volume by volume our haunted house grows. Enter at your own risk!

Pulling Back the Curtain

Spirits Between the Bays series—Vol. I

The first book of the *Spirits Between the Bays* ghost/folkore series includes more than a dozen Mid-Atlantic ghost tales, including the Curse of Blackbeard's Treasure, the Revolutionary War's Headless Horseman of Welsh Tract Road and the Ghost of Ashley Manor, which the author visited the week before Halloween.

"*In Pulling Back the Curtain by Ed Okonowicz, the Cecil County resident doesn't have to go far to find ghosts.*" —Baltimore Sun

"*The stories are even more fascinating for local readers because Okonowicz interviewed Delmarva residents for the book.*" — Cecil Whig [Elkton, Md.]

"*Okonowicz collects, refines and tells interesting legends and folktales that have been passed by families from generation to generation.*" —Newark Post [Newark, Del.]

Opening the Door

Spirits Between the Bays series—Vol. II

(second edition)

This volume includes more than 20 ghost tales, including the spirits of Woodburn, Delaware's Governor's Mansion; Elmer Tyson: Eastern Shore Gravedigger; the Bleeding Stone of White House Farm; a spirit-infested mobile home; restless souls at a Delaware River oil refinery; the murder of slaves near the Mason-Dixon Line; ghostly guardian angels floating in the sky, and many more true incidents and legends.

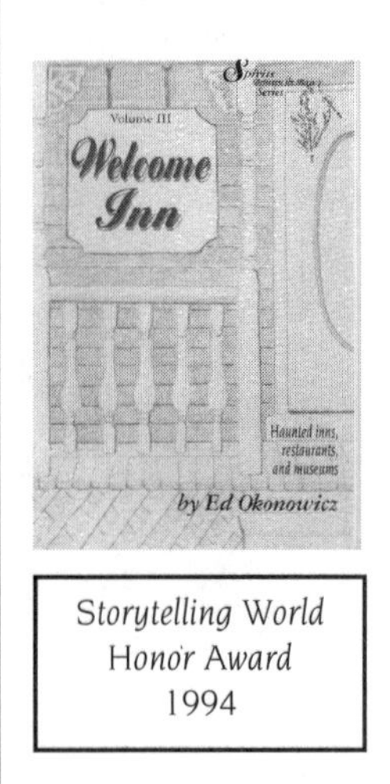

Storytelling World Honor Award 1994

Welcome Inn

Spirits Between the Bays series—Vol. III

Welcome Inn series features true stories of unusual events at 13 public sites—including restaurants, inns and museums—visited by people every day. We invite the daring, the curious and especially the skeptics, to take a spirited trip across the peninsula—from the Chadds Ford Inn in Pennsylvania, to the Blue Coat Inn in Dover, to a pair of haunted inns in Snow Hill, Maryland, and in Fort Delaware's Civil War dungeons . . . plus other sites. Make your reservations to dine at a haunted table, stay overnight in a ghost room or tour a mysterious museum. Who knows what chills you will experience . . . what phantoms you will meet?

"*. . . a sort of auto-club guide to ghosts, spirits and the unexplainable by* Ed Okonowicz, *a free-lance writer and ghost junkie.*" — Washington Times/Associated Press

In the Vestibule

Spirits Between the Bays series—Vol. IV

This book includes 15 true tales about a wide range of unusual creatures, including haunted horses at a thoroughbred stable on Maryland's Eastern Shore, a ghost infested hotel in New Jersey, Bigfoot's visits to Maryland, sightings of the Snallygaster, the story of Delmarva's first serial killer—the notorious Patty Cannon—and many more.

From Avalon and Ocean City in New Jersey, to Lewes and Wilmington in Delaware and in Baltimore, Reliance and Easton in Maryland, the dead still walk at night.

"*If this collection doesn't give you a chill, check your pulse, you might be dead.*" — The Review [University of Delaware]

"*The 15 stories, mostly creepy, in In the Vestibule, include one about Patty Cannon...*" — Star Democrat [Easton, Md.]

Delaware Press Association First Place Award 1997

Presence in the Parlor

Spirits Between the Bays series—Vol. V

Delaware Press Association
First Place Award
1998

Features 19 true ghost stories and two popular legends. The chapters include tales of haunted Indian sites, ghosts in Baltimore Harbor on the USS *Constellation*, a floating casket that comes home to rest in Accomack County, Va., ghost stories from Tangier Island, the "Dream Lady" in Talbot County, Md., and haunted inns in New Castle, Del., and Salem, N.J.

"Okonowicz lulls the reader into a false sense of security and then—Wham!—he hits you with some terrifying detail..."
— Chris Woodyard, Invisible Ink

"So make some hot chocolate, turn out the lights, light some candles and read this local ghost story aloud."
— The Sentinel-Ledger [Ocean City, N.J.]

Crying in the Kitchen

Spirits Between the Bays series—Vol. VI

Delaware Press Association
First Place Award
1999

This book focuses on ghost stories based on interviews with residents of Mid-Atlantic watertowns—such as Cape May, Lewes, Chincoteague, Salem, New Hope and Rehoboth Beach. Read about the headless phantom on Smith Island in the Chesapeake Bay and learn about ghosts featured on the evening Lantern Tours at the old Civil War prison at Fort Delaware on Pea Patch Island. Discover details on the submerged city of Conowingo, the Weather Witch that protects a sunken treasure ship, the Unknown Sailors' Cemetery under the Lewes Ferry Terminal parking lot and the mass graves of Confederate prisoners at Fort Mott National Cemetery. . . and more.

"...when the lights go down, just remember, watch out for what is—or isn't—behind you!"
— Delaware River and Bay Authority Traveler

"Hidden slaves left to die in a secret passage, a Lewes parking lot built over a graveyard..." — Dover Post [Dover, Del.]

"Okonowicz's new book is much different than the others in that it highlights only 'coast ghosts'..." — Beachcomber [Ocean City, Md.]

Visit our web site at: www.mystandlace.com

Up the Back Stairway

Spirits Between the Bays series—Vol. VII

This book features 26 stories of Mid-Atlantic haunts, including demonic spirits in Salem County, N.J., ghosts in Pennsylvania's Red Rose Inn and strange events in Virginia's Oak Spring Farm, plus the legend of the Ticking Tomb, mysterious melodies from Fiddler's Bridge, ghostly pirates on the Jersey Shore, a vampire tale set on the Eastern Shore of Maryland. . . and more.

Delaware Press Association Second Place Award 2000

"DON'T *read these stories alone, late at night, in the dead of winter, when no one can hear your screams.*"
— Port Deposit Post [Port Deposit, Md.]

Horror in the Hallway

Spirits Between the Bays series—Vol. VIII

Terror awaits at every page turn as readers progress through this eighth volume of the *Spirits Between the Bays* ghost/folklore series. These 28 tales are from people living in Pennsylvania, Maryland, New Jersey and Delaware. All have experienced the unexplained and share their stories about the curse of a deadly violin, the evil occupant of an antique bed, a jinxed bungalow, the haunted jail in Denton, Md., restless slave ghosts in a Pennsylvania farmhouse and the long hidden horror associated with the Pink House. . . . and more.

Phantom in the Bedchamber

Spirits Between the Bays series Vol. IX

Civil War ghosts and haunted lighthouses are the focus of this volume. Learn of the spirits in Gettysburg's Farnsworth House Inn and Restaurant and the ghosts at Point Lookout State Park (at one time site of the nation's largest Civil War prison). Readers also will encounter and enjoy eerie tales associated with a graveyard near Easton, Maryland, ghostly activity in two Delaware businesses, ghost hunters in New Jersey, what it's like to move a corpse and the strange encounters at "the most haunted lighthouse in America," located at the southern tip of Maryland's Western Shore.

Nearly 20 stories are included in this terrifying volume, and eight of the sites are open to the public—the most listed in any volume since Welcome Inn, Vol. III, our very popular book on haunted inns restaurants and museums.

Matt Zabitka: Sports
60 Years of Headlines and Deadlines

by Ed Okonowicz and Jerry Rhodes

224 pages
over 30 photographs
6" x 9"
ISBN 1-890690-09-0
hardbound
$24.95

Since his first hand-written column for Chester's *Progressive Weekly* at age 13, Matt "Zee" Zabitka has been associated with professional, scholastic and amateur sports. In more than 10,000 columns, Zee has shared his conversations with sports' greatest legends and he has recorded the achievements of local heroes.

This book features scores of Matt's favorite experiences and more than 35 columns, which he has selected—including interviews with Joe DiMaggio, Stan Musial, "Boom Boom" Mancini, Ted Williams, Goose Goslin and Ralph Kiner. There also are columns about local athletes plus a section spotlighting Delawareans who played in the Negro National Baseball League.

Read about Matt's personal correspondence with Ty Cobb, his stint as a radio show host and his experiences as a sought after toastmaster.

Following 10 years at the *Chester Times*, the "classic" sportswriter joined *The News Journal* in 1962 and has never stopped writing.

This hardbound book will be a collector's item.

Matt, as described by others in the field of sports

"When I first met him, he immediately struck me as the classic sportswriter. If they were going to do a movie about Matt's life, it's a shame that Walter Matthau died, because he could play Matt—with a cigar hanging halfway out of his mouth, banging on a typewriter, talking on the phone and working late into the night." **—Kevin Tresolini,** sportswriter, *The News Journal*

"Every city of any size needs a Matt Zabitka, who I respectfully call a chronicler, someone who has a history and picture of the past. You need someone with deep roots in the community. Wilmington is fortunate to have that in Matt."
—Pat Williams, senior vice president, Orlando Magic

"He made you feel comfortable, and he made me feel important. He's been kind to me and he's always covered my career in a positive way. That means a lot to me. He's a really good guy."
—Randy White, former defensive tackle for the Dallas Cowboys and member of the Pro Football Hall of Fame

 Visit our web site at: www.mystandlace.com

The DelMarVa Murder Mystery series

FIRED!

320 pages
4 1/4" x 6 3/4"
softcover
ISBN 1-890690-01-5

$9.95

Early in the 21st century, DelMarVa, the newest state in the union, which includes Delaware and the Eastern Shore of Maryland and Virginia, is plagued by a ruthless serial killer. In FIRED! meet Gov. Henry McDevitt, Police Commissioner Michael Pentak and State Psychologist Stephanie Litera as they track down the peninsula's worst killer since 19th century murderess Patty Cannon.

"Politics and romance make fairly strange bedfellows, but add a dash of mystery and mahem and the result can be spectacular, as evidenced in FIRED!"

—Sharon Galligar Chance
BookBrowser Review

Delaware Press Association First Place Award 1999

". . . this is Okonowicz's best book so far!"

—The Star Democrat
Easton, Md.

Halloween House

320 pages
4 1/4" x 6 3/4"
softcover
ISBN 1-890690-03-1

$9.95

In *Halloween House*, the series continues as Gov. McDevitt, Commissioner Pentak and other DelMarVa crime fighters go up against Craig Dire, a demented businessman who turns his annual Halloween show into a real-life chamber of horrors.

National Federation of Press Women First Place Award 2000

"Halloween House *mystery chills summer heat."*

—Rosanne Pack
Cape Gazette

"Looking at the front cover, the reader knows it's going to be a bumpy night."

—Erika Quesenbery
The Herald

Visit our web site at: www.mystandlace.com

Disappearing Delmarva

Portraits of the Peninsula People

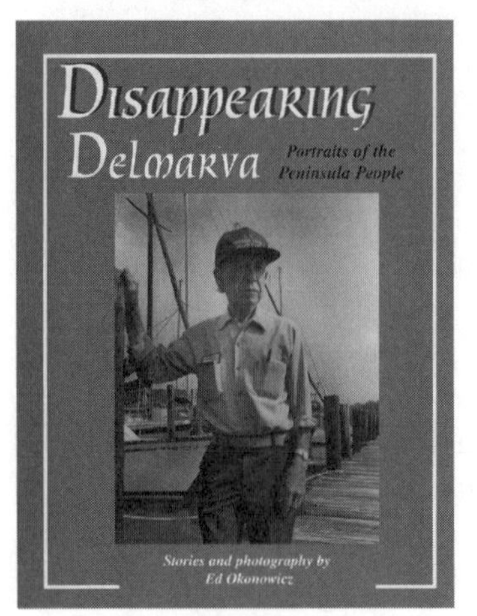

Photography and stories
by Ed Okonowicz

Disappearing Delmarva introduces you to more than 70 people on the peninsula whose professions are endangered. Their work, words and wisdom are captured in the 208 pages of this hardbound volume, which features more than 60 photographs.

Along the back roads and back creeks of Delaware, Maryland, and Virginia—in such hamlets as Felton and Blackbird in Delaware, Taylors Island and North East in Maryland, and Chincoteague and Sanford in Virginia—these colorful residents still work at the trades that have been passed down to them by grandparents and elders.

208 pages
8 1/2" x 11"
Hardcover
ISBN 1-890690-00-7

$38.00

Winner of 2 First-Place Awards:

Best general book
Best Photojournalism entry

National Federation of Press Women Inc.

1998 Communication Contest

Ed presents a program based on this award-winning book at local historical societies and libraries. Contact him at 410 398-5013 to arrange a program in your area.

 Visit our web site at:www.mystandlace.com

Friends, Neighbors and Folks Down the Road

Photography and stories by
Ed Okonowicz & Jerry Rhodes

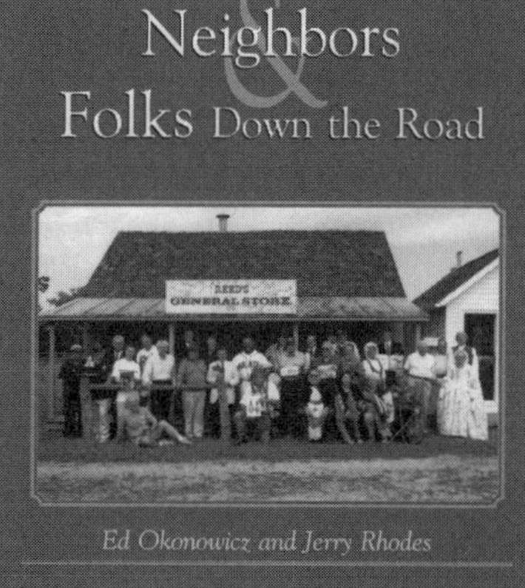

Meet the "Gnome Man," "The Master Foul Ball Chaser," a couple who collected 2 million signatures to get the POW/MIA stamp issued, an artist who met with Oprah Winfrey, the "Jefferson Letter Lady," the "Bubble Man" and a U.S. Coast Guard photographer who took pictures on the beach on D-Day.

These are only a few of the 58 *Friends, Neighbors and Folks Down the Road* who are featured in this coffee-table style, hardbound volume.

208 pages
8 1/2" x 11"
Hardcover
ISBN 1-890690-12-0

$30.00

From small towns and cities in Lancaster County, Pa., Cecil County, Md., and New Castle, Kent and Sussex counties in Delaware, there are dozens of unique, surprising and entertaining characters waiting to be discovered and seen in the stories and nearly 150 photographs in this book. They all prove that there are fascinating people worth knowing about, who are located right down the road and around the bend.

". . . fun-to-read coffee-table book"

—*Delaware Today Magazine*

" Reading the first chapter is like finding a $20 bill in the pocket of your jeans on laundry day; unexpected, a pleasant surprise, an omen of good things to come."

—David Healey, *The Cecil Whig*

To complete your collection. . .

or to tell us about *your* ghostly experience, use the form below:

Name ____________________

Address ____________________

City ____________________ State __________ Zip Code __________

Phone Numbers _(_____)____________________ (_____)____________________
Day Evening

To receive the free *Spirits Speaks* newsletter and information on future volumes, public tours and events, send us your e-mail address, visit our web site [www.mystandlace.com] or fill out the above form and mail it to us.

I would like to order the following books:

Quantity	Title	Price	Total
______	**Terrifying Tales of the Beaches and Bays**	**$ 9.95**	______
______	Terrifying Tales 2 of the Beaches and Bays	$ 9.95	______
______	Treasure Hunting	$ 6.95	______
______	Pulling Back the Curtain, Vol I	$ 8.95	______
______	Opening the Door, Vol II (second edition)	$ 9.95	______
______	Welcome Inn, Vol III	$ 8.95	______
______	In the Vestibule, Vol IV	$ 9.95	______
______	Presence in the Parlor, Vol V	$ 9.95	______
______	Crying in the Kitchen, Vol VI	$ 9.95	______
______	Up the Back Stairway, Vol VII	$ 9.95	______
______	Horror in the Hallway, Vol VIII	$ 9.95	______
______	Phantom in the Bedchamber, Vol IX	$ 9.95	______
______	Possessed Possessions	$ 9.95	______
______	Possessed Possessions 2	$ 9.95	______
______	Ghosts	$ 9.95	______
______	Fired! A DelMarVa Murder Mystery (DMM)	$ 9.95	______
______	Halloween House (DMM#2)	$ 9.95	______
______	Disappearing Delmarva	$38.00	______
______	Friends, Neighbors & Folks Down the Road	$30.00	______
______	Stairway over the Brandywine, A Love Story	$ 5.00	______
______	Matt Zabitka: Sports	$24.95	______

*Md residents add 5% sales tax.
Please include $2.00 postage for the first book, and 50 cents for each additional book.
Make checks payable to:
Myst and Lace Publishers

Subtotal __________
Tax* __________
Shipping __________
Total __________

All books are signed by the author. If you would like the book(s) personalized, please specify to whom.

Mail to: Ed Okonowicz
1386 Fair Hill Lane
Elkton, Maryland 21921

 Visit our web site at: www.mystandlace.com